The Heart's Precision

THE HEART'S PRECISION

Judson Crews and his Poetry

by

WENDELL ANDERSON

Edited and with a bibliography of Judson Crews by

JEFFERSON P. SELTH

310 327 8219

DUMONT PRESS

Published by Dumont Press
P.O. Box 11081
Carson CA 90749-1081

Publisher's cataloging information:

Anderson, Wendell.
 The heart's precision; Judson Crews and his poetry. Edited and
with a bibliography of Judson Crews by Jefferson P. Selth.
  p. cm.
Includes bibliographical references and index.
 1. Crews, Judson, 1917-   I. Selth, Jefferson P. II. Title.
PS3553.R47Z   811   94-71189
           ISBN 0-9624431-5-8

Cover photograph:
"Self Image" by Judson Crews

Printed in the United States of America

Contents

APPENDIX: A BIBLIOGRAPHY OF JUDSON CREWS

PART 1

A Life

Introduction

In 1943 Judson Crews addressed a letter to a young poet acquaintance by the name of Wendell Anderson, who was living and working on a wildlife refuge high up on a mountain in the deserts of southeastern Oregon with his young wife. "Nine months," he wrote, he had been in Oregon and had "just begun to realize that Wendell Anderson was there." So Judson, my wife Dodie and I met in Portland. Dodie and I had left the refuge with our infant son and returned to the city so that I could resume my studies at Reed College.

Judson came from Camp Adair at Corvallis, Oregon, dressed very simply in his army uniform, a clean-cut young man with high cheek bones, a generous mouth and broad Texas accent. He was a very handsome man, and we plunged immediately into talk about our writing and reading. J.C. Crews, as simple and clean and forthright as that....

Childhood and Youth

The pulse of the child unborn is a soft insistent beat beneath the mother's abdomen. Insistent and almost one with the mother's. The heartbeat when amplified has a rhythmic, almost hard beat. If amplified loudly enough it can fill a room with sound. Without amplification it can fill the world. The heartbeat. The sound could be a drumbeat. The pulse of drums beating in the dances of the Indians of the Southwest, firm strokes on hard leather, all day under the Southwest sun. Drums beating and voices chanting in prayer for the rain. There are also the drums of war that beat loud and insistent. These too fill the world.

Judson Campbell Crews was born on June 30th, 1917, a few months after the United States entered World War I. He was born in Waco, Texas, of Noah George Crews, a nurseryman, and Tommie (Farmer) Crews, the last child of a large family. The religious background was Southern Bible Belt, particularly through his mother. She was a rather tall woman of strong character, the kind that evokes the thought of the "pioneer woman and mother." The father was hard-working and hard-driving, especially in the use of his sons working on the fifty acres that comprised the nursery. As a boy from the age of nine, the poet spent many long hours weeding unending rows. It was the sons who cemented in the loads and loads of rock that went into the construction of the rock gardens of the nursery, a showplace in Waco.

The ancestry of the family was Scotch-Irish, as American a background as can be found. Southern as far back as there is. They were apparently from either Tennessee or the Carolinas, and came westward very early in the history of Texas to the Brazos country. I have it on the authority of a member of the family very close to Judson (not a word from the poet himself) that it was "one of the first families in and of Texas." The children were all tall and strongly built, with well-modulated bone structure. The complexion was fair, very clear-skinned. Beautiful strong white teeth and dark hair—if not black, as in the case of the poet and his brothers—could attest to the strong Irish strain. Upon occasion Judson himself has said, "Of course I'm Irish, too."

Of his father he wrote:

> My father was an orphan almost from birth. His mother
> had two sons and another husband after he was born, and
> even then died in the seventh month of another pregnancy
> at nineteen.
>
> And he was dragged all over the middle plains of Texas
> by an erratic uncle and his poor wife, trotting hound-
> fashion behind the big double-yoke ox-cart, kicking up dry
> cow turds with his bare toes. I suppose he had enough to
> eat, and they settled sometimes for long enough to raise a
> crop of tobacco which he helped cure and chewed. He got
> in a few semesters of grammar school edgewise, excelling
> in penmanship, spelling and mathematics. Later he was at
> Georgetown College, or somewhere now dead, taking busi-
> ness, bookkeeping and accounting, which he never used.
>
> He fell in with a journeyman photographer who kept
> contracting bad accounts. They wound up in Mexia, Texas,
> where he met my mother. They married and fled to Waco
> and started raising prize chickens and kids. My mother
> never even got to go home (fifty miles) for eleven years,
> they were so poor. My grandmother came for a few weeks
> when there was a new child to be born.[1]

> I was born on a fifty-acre fruit and vegetable farm about
> three miles from Waco, Texas, in 1917. I grew up like a
> stunted weed and at seven went to a three-room, eight-
> grade school for four years. That summer my tonsils were
> removed with the money my mother had worked to save
> for over two years. I went to a consolidated school.[2]

Many references to his boyhood are scattered through his writings.
A particularly poignant short story, "The Beginning of Remembrance,"[3]
was about a boyhood friend. Another poem, "Pictures of Sixteen,"
gives us a vivid picture of the social as well as emotional conditions of
a boy's adolescence during the grim Depression years. Judson was fifteen years of age in 1932.

A passage from his poem "The River" acquaints the reader with the power of boyhood reminiscence:

> Why ever name the word again
> once Joyce has written Plurabelle
> swollen and mumbling every name
> from Styx to Stong
>   with every leaf
> and odour, and branch
> and root and ripple even to the gurgling urinal and
> the stench of the sewers of Paris
> and the odour of honey on the bee's breeze
> Surely he has squeezed them dry
> to the bone rock necessity of silence
> yet I remember naked boys in a sow wallow
> in the Brazos bottom
> with bone rock penises and a captive sow
> dumb to the river but sounding out
> their swollen concept of carnal sin
> Has one of them found Joyce to this day
> though still awake to carnal sin
> yet never remembering the blasting sun
> nor the honey pervading the sultry air
> nor even the flesh
>   only when they tumble
> a whore or their wife
> and not even then, only the vague revulsion
> murmuring quietly sin, sin, sin

In all outward aspects his boyhood would seem to have been that of the normal child, an outdoor life close to the soil, but it was a spare and frugal life. There were children to support. The home was somewhat grim. A certain moody, explosive quality may have been an undercurrent within the family flow of life. He was the youngest child, closest perhaps to his mother and to one or two of his sisters. His hand was needed in the fields and he began his chores, as did his brothers, at the rows of weeds and at the rockpile. These were the Depression years—slow years, described in "Pictures of Sixteen":

The sky's moving slow today
it's moving like a nation
that's got culture
pulsing deep in its veins
like a nation that's got a past
that glory ain't no name for
a nation that's got a past but ain't got
charity (the preacher said read love)

Ain't gonna have no future
He didn't say it
His lips quivered and he
looked at the buzzard and said:
Brother!
except God gave you wings....

He began writing poetry as a child, as early as eight or nine, but it was not until the eighth grade that he began to write with deliberate intent. He first tried a novel, *A Romantic Western*, then went on to poetry the following year.

He was sixteen when in 1933 he discovered the "New Poetry" of Carl Sandburg, Amy Lowell and Edgar Lee Masters:

Sandburg affected me strangely. When I first read *The New Poetry* at sixteen, he was almost certainly my ideal. During the next two or three years I read all I could get of his *Chicago Poems, Smoke and Steel, Cornhuskers*, and one other. I was thrilled. I knew he was the greatest. Certainly greater than Lindsay, Masters or Frost. And I was pretty sure he was greater than Robinson, whom I hadn't read. I made a 150-mile trip when I didn't have any money and needed rest to see him on a platform and hear him. I was thrilled. I said he was ageless. That was in November 1937, one year after my father committed suicide. I saw him again in August 1938, at Boulder, where I had gone without money enough to eat on, and without knowledge enough to get some work so I could eat. He and Elmer Rice and Eric Knight (who is dead) had a meeting to

discuss the Spanish Civil War. They spoke of Peace. There
was no *reason* why I shouldn't have been thrilled but I
wasn't. Paul Engle was there too. I knew, then, I don't
know how, that Sandburg wasn't ageless. I saw Engle, "a
matinee darling," and knew his heart didn't have any
anger. I wanted still, I don't know why, to buy *The People,
Yes*, but I didn't have the money. Later I could and no
longer wanted to. I saw Macleish make an about face and
my heart went sick in me. Dos Passos wrote *The Ground
We Stand On*, but in writing it he got off the ground he
stood on. I am glad Sherwood Anderson is dead. Though
I still have enough illusion to think he would have stood,
though he had to stand alone.[4]

Judson graduated from La Vega High School at Bellmead, Texas, in
1935, at the age of seventeen, playing tackle on the football team in his
senior year.

I finished high school and for two years lived submerged working for my father...who committed suicide in November of '36.
I started at Baylor University the next fall.[2]

Intending to take courses in Baylor's Bible Department, he was
accepted in the fall of 1937. He quit before the year was over, after
launching a mimeographed magazine called *Vers Libre*. He returned to
the University the following fall, 1938, to start a double major in
English and Sociology and a double minor in Psychology and Social
Sciences. He says that during this time he made three or four friends,
the first since high school. He received his A.B. in the summer of 1941
and began work on an M.A. in the fall of the same year.

We have a vivid portrait of the young Judson Crews at Baylor
University from a reminiscence of Scott Greer:

I have known Mr. Crews since 1941 when he was an undergraduate at Baylor University. At that time he was the
most brilliant student in the Sociology Department and
was also the literary figure on the campus. He was a pro-
tégé of the dramatist Lynn Riggs.... He had already pub-

lished poetry and prose rather widely...as well as winning, rather consistently, the literary prizes offered by the University....[5]

He had abandoned *Vers Libre* by this time and founded another magazine called *Motive*, which merged a year later with *Iconograph* under the editorship of Kenneth Lawrence Beaudoin in New Orleans. Beaudoin is another fascinating literary figure from the avant-garde poetry of the early 1930s to the 1960s. Of Judson he wrote:

> I first became acquainted with Judson Crews in 1933[6] through *Vers Libre*, a little magazine of which he was editor which came out of Waco, Texas. *Vers Libre* was a little mimeographed magazine which seemed to have a freshness to it, which I found very engaging. We were all young then and madly in pursuit of some redeeming beauty which would be our salvation. And perhaps a little more interesting salvation than the Bible Belt mores we had been bred to provided. We were, I guess, the first group of flower children in the South, though we referred to ourselves as bohemians, and our hair never got quite as long as it seems to nowadays. Of course, haircuts were cheaper then. And, of course, we drank beer and bourbon and did not use marijuana or pep pills. It was an exciting period for us, however, for somehow all of us felt we were entering a new period of human awareness which at least had not happened before in the South and the Southwest. We wrote much of love, still in the Southern romantic tradition, and of the sad lot of tenant farmers and other submerged groups we encountered in what is now referred to as the Great Depression in the United States. I don't know that we were more earnest or more distinguished than any other group of young American poets, but the poems which appeared in *Vers Libre, Iconograph* and *Crescendo* in that period before World War II, were unique. Judson Crews, Scott Greer, Oscar Collier and a number of others including myself found our identities as poets during that period.

Judson Crews visited me once while I was in New Orleans in the '30s. I found him a raw-boned young man from Texas full of all sorts of reticences I did not find in the New Orleans group I was associated with then.

Then there was World War II and the subsequent disorientation that followed. I found myself in New York where *Iconograph* and I had moved and where I operated a little art gallery called Galerie Neuf in East 79th Street, closer to the East River than to the Metropolitan Museum. It is odd that the impact of the War did not seem to produce any great body of work from any of us. As a matter of fact, it seemed to silence us for a while. It was not until several years after World War II that any of us started writing again, i.e. for publication. We wrote during the war period, but nothing that we seemed to want to submit to public print. It was in the period after the War that I wrote my *2 Suites for Manhattan*. And it was in this immediately post-war period that Crews came to New York, married Mildred Tolbert, a superb photographer, and then decided to return to Ranches of Taos where they lived for so many years publishing *Motive* and operating the Motive Book Shop.[7]

I published Judson Crews' first collection of poems, *Psalms for a Late Season*, while *Iconograph* was still in New Orleans. I do not have a copy of it to refer to anymore, but I remember that we thought it a fine piece of work and one of the better pieces published by Iconograph Press. In the early '50s I used to receive many of the little Motive Press editions of Judson Crews' poems.[8]

The War Years

War Year: 1943

No hell of trail
cut to our making
we came through, came through
buffeted by hours
lean men buffeted by time

Lean hunger nursing us
on these long trails
we cut them through
cut them through
through the teeming jungle
there to the restless sea

No ships and men
the beaches strewn, we found
the trail at end
the hunger at end
we found our end
down at the restless sea

Judson volunteered for war service in the spring of 1942, and was made a staff sergeant in the Medical Corps. While in training he was transferred from one army camp to another, writing to his friends from Camp Horn, Arizona, Camp Adair, Oregon, and four places in California: Beaumont, Camp Blythe, Camp Young at Indio, and San Bernardino.

His favorite authors were now Sherwood Anderson, Vardis Fisher, Henry Miller and D.H. Lawrence. He himself had not written anything for a year, but he was corresponding and maintaining literary contacts. He furnished booklists, and quite frequently sent books, to these correspondents. He traveled with a duffle bag full of books, and maintained his Motive Book Shop of avant-garde literature through correspondence—"on the fly," so to speak. He introduced various of his friends to a whole world of reading by referring to Henry Miller, Vardis Fisher, Anaïs Nin, Jean Giono, Kenneth Patchen, Jacob Wasserman, Count Herman Von Keyserling, Wilhelm Stekel and many others.[9]

It was during this time that he met Henry Miller in Los Angeles. It was a memorable experience, which he has described vividly in a memoir of his year with Miller.[10]

In May 1943 he had been hospitalized with gastritis, and in January 1944 the condition returned. There followed a miserable period in which he was in one army hospital after another, undergoing tests and medical examinations. This lasted a month, and he passed through not only a physical ordeal but an emotional crisis as well. It was, in a sense, a kind of rebirth. On March 2, 1944 he wrote briefly: "The worst is passed. I know without having a reason for knowing it." He was subsequently medically discharged and left the service in April 1944 for Waco. The War was still raging.

He resumed as a graduate student at Baylor University in late May. He was regaining his health slowly, though still suffering from fatigue, and finding it difficult to concentrate on the work he wanted to complete.

At Baylor he found his old friends Scott Greer, Dr. and Mrs. Kinsinger and their daughter Delia, Meredith Weatherby and others. He spent almost eight hours a day on his Master's thesis in sociology, which Scott Greer typed up for him when completed. 550 pages long, its title was *The Treatment of Social Problems in Recent Southern Literature*. He wrote:

> If the thesis is published, it will be under some other title than *The Treatment of Social Problems in Recent Southern Literature*.... Any suggestions would be welcome! I thought of *The Southern Temper; A Literary Analysis* but that itself is not too good, though much better than the original title.[11]

He received an M.A. With Honor.

By October 1944 he was planning to leave Waco and travel up the California coast to Big Sur, Monterey, and possibly Portland. He arrived in Portland in October, and with Scott Greer, who had

preceded him there a month earlier, found employment in the Post
Office Department. After three months, in January 1945, he left for Big
Sur. He was bearded and wore long hair. Henry Miller, who was living
in a cabin on Partington Ridge at Big Sur, wrote years later:

> Judson Crews of Waco, Texas, one of the first to muscle
> in, reminded one because of his shaggy beard and manner
> of speech of a latter-day prophet. He lived almost exclu-
> sively on peanut butter and wild mustard greens and nei-
> ther smoked nor drank.[12]

In addition to Henry and his beautiful young wife, Marta Lepska,
and his secretary, Emil White, there was at Big Sur and in adjoining
Carmel and Monterey a group of writers and artists. One was John
McKinney, a sculptor, who lived with his mistress and baby son Jerry,
and who was later to become a legendary figure in the art colonies of
Taos and Santa Fe, and one of the closest friends of Judson and
Mildred Crews.

Another resident of the area was George Leite, a young energetic
poet, who edited *Circle*, one of the most unusual avant-garde magazines
of the World War II era. He published a number of fine issues, all
appearing in an interesting and artistic format, presenting many of the
best writers, poets and artists of the period. Judson Crews, Lawrence
Durrell, Henry Miller, William Everson (Brother Antoninus), Alex
Comfort, Walker Winslow, Hilaire Hiler, Elwood Graham, Harold
Norse, Selwyn Schwartz, Byron Vazakas, Harry Roskolenko, Michael
Fraenkel, Paul Radin, Kenneth Patchen, Josephine Miles, Philip
Lamantia, Nicholas Moore, Weldon Kees, Anaïs Nin, Wallace Fowlie,
James Franklin Lewis and Kenneth Rexroth all figured among the con-
tributors.[13]

This was a restless period for Judson. He lived at Big Sur for about
four months, then worked as a fire guard on the Malheur National Forest at John Day, Oregon, during the long, hot summer of 1945.

The first atomic bomb was dropped on Hiroshima on August 6,
1945. He had been fighting fire every weekend, almost without pause,
for it had been one of the worst forest fire seasons in the Northwest
in thirty years. By August the health he had regained while resting in
Waco had been used up, and the gastric condition that had plagued him

in the Army returned. He resigned from the Forest Service and left
again for Big Sur. The war was over on August 15. His poem "Many
Islands" is eloquent in its elegiac mood:

> I never said that summer was a sword
> I never said that all the soldiers would be dead
>
> The moon rises in summer as in winter
> no bayonet yet has spiked it for long
>
> Oh our season, our season, prismatic as time
> our time pragmatic as love. The moon
>
> Left debris in its wake on many islands
> on many islands the soldiers lie
>
> They lie in the arms of the memory of mercy
> they lie as if smitten with the memory of love
>
> But it was not the memory that did it here
> nor was it the summer's cruel sword

He returned to Big Sur via Walla Walla, Washington and Berkeley.
Alternately hitchhiking and traveling by bus. He wrote on August 27
from Big Sur:

> Just a note as it is almost time for the mail.
> I made it alright though I slept one night in the jail in
> Pacific Grove and toted my baggage half way from Big Sur
> to Anderson Creek.

At Big Sur, in this immediate post-war period, he began writing
again, in what he has called "a primarily imagistic mode." His friends
were Henry Miller, the Leites, Norman Mini, Varda, Gilbert and
Margaret Neiman, and many others of the artists and writers there.

He left Big Sur for Waco on December 16, 1945. In the winter and
spring of 1946 he wrote a novel and a book of poetry, the poetry
representing a breakthrough to a more "metaphysical dimension." He

sent the novel to Henry Miller, who thought it so poor (though he had earlier praised Judson's poetry and Master's thesis[14]) that the young man thought of abandoning his writing altogether.

In the meanwhile Dorothy Norman had accepted a group of the poems for *Twice a Year*, and Caresse Crosby a group for *Portfolio*. Both magazines discontinued publication before they appeared. After he had learned to print in Taos, he published the "best half" of them in *No Is The Night*.

Taos

Absolution

I have returned
where returning was untenable

I left
the bleak wild coast

Can you not understand
that willing
is not necessarily being

Not being is the only absolute state

Can you not understand
the course of water over stone
for a thousand years

I got to Waco a few days before Christmas and have been here at home ever since. The Veterans' Administration here has promised to give me action on my claims not later than the middle of March. If they do I can get to New York in time to enter spring quarter at the School of Social Work at Columbia.

...Finally got an acceptance from *New Mexico Quarterly
Review* after rejection of one hundred poems from twenty-
five magazines.[15]

This was a period of restlessness. Apart from one last visit to Big Sur
in May 1946 lasting only three weeks, he remained in Waco until June
1947, studying art at Baylor University, though illness forced him to
drop out during the winter.

He was both selling and publishing books, calling his business Motive Press and Motive Book Shop. Dismayed to discover that a California publisher had issued Henry Miller's 64-page essay *Maurizius Forever*
at ten dollars a copy, he republished it at a price the public could
afford: 65 cents. At the same time he was selling a small book of his
own poems for ten cents, a price so ridiculously low that Kathryn
Winslow thought of advising him to raise it to twenty cents or even a
quarter.[16]

One of his most regular customers was Henry Miller. Almost all of
Miller's letters express deep appreciation to Judson, either for his
personal friendship or for the immense amount of time he put into
"business" on Henry's behalf. Miller was constantly asking him to look
out for a copy of a book, sometimes one of his own to give or sell to
a friend, more often a work by another author of whom he was currently enamored. Usually he found the book very quickly, eliciting
from Henry the most generous expressions of gratitude and sometimes
astonishment. He would also, on his own initiative, locate copies of
Miller's books that were still illegally circulating in the United States
and lend them to his friends, a gesture Henry called unprecedented in
his experience.[17]

Finally he went to Taos to study art with Dr. Kinsinger, his Baylor
professor. It was here that he met Mildred.

The meeting of the poet Judson Crews and the photographer Mildred Tolbert almost seems to have been prearranged by fate. He had
rented an apartment in an old picturesque adobe house on La Loma in
Taos for some 33 dollars a month, where he lived frugally, as always.
One day he passed the office of a Dr. Dominguez. In one of the windows was a display of photographs by a woman named Mildred Tolbert. He was astonished to see portraits of his New York friends Oscar
Collier and Kenneth Lawrence Beaudoin. The photographer's phone

number was listed in the display. His curiosity aroused, he called the number. Mildred answered the phone and heard a "strange Texas drawl." They were married in Taos on October 19, 1947.

He began to write prolifically. By the time they left for New York in December 1947 he had completed three hundred poems. Hayden Carruth accepted a group of them for *Poetry* magazine. Henry Rago, the magazine's head, was one of the few established editors (as opposed to the little magazines) to publish his work.

The newly married couple lived in a tenement on New York's lower East Side, trying to make ends meet. It was difficult to find employment, and Judson worked in a box factory for 30 dollars a week, and as a market research assistant.

They met a number of artists and writers in the city, among them Michael Fraenkel, Harry Hershkowitz, Maxwell Bodenheim, Lee Ver Duft, and their old friends Kenneth Lawrence Beaudoin, Oscar Collier and Gertrude Barer.

His employment in the box factory was undependable, sometimes for only one day a week. He scoured the want ads, but nothing turned up. A baby was due in August. In this bleak situation they returned to Taos, where their first daughter, Anna Bush Crews, was born on September 18, 1948. The summer and fall of this year were especially productive poetically; in these months he produced a large segment of what he considers to be both his best and his poorest work.

He found self-employment under the G.I. Bill, which gave him 100 dollars a month. Later, a VA "on-the-job program" provided him and his wife and the infant daughter with scarcely a living wage. He worked in the mechanical department of the Taos *Star* and learned printing and linotype operation. He planned, by means of the trade he was learning, to print a number of booklets of poetry, including one of his own. *No is the Night*—a beautifully printed pamphlet, his first collection in seven years—appeared in 1949 under his own imprint: Motive Book Shop, Route 7, Box 613, Waco, Texas.

He had also resumed publishing his poetry magazines; in all he was to publish and edit nine such journals over a period of 20 years.[18] As Kathryn Winslow has testified,[19] when most poetry magazines were accepting work only from established poets, several edited by Judson were full of poems by newcomers. His Motive Press also published collections of poems by Michael Fraenkel, Wendell Anderson and Scott Greer.

The year 1949 was marked by the purchase of an old adobe house in Ranches of Taos. A rambling building of twelve or thirteen rooms, it dated back two hundred or more years in parts of its structure. It was located in a quiet rural section, near the famous St. Francis of Assisi Church. Gardens, fields, irrigation ditches, fruit trees, with the mountains looming beyond.

There followed a series of problems. The *Star* died, but he found employment within a few weeks at *El Crepusculo*, another Taos newspaper. A second daughter, Carole Judith Crews, was born July 7, 1950. The two girls grew up in the old house at Ranches of Taos.

The years at this location were times of heavy physical labor for Judson. He stood on a concrete floor 40 to 48 hours a week—or even more when work was pressing. There was little time for leisure or creative work. He never had more than a few days of vacation a year, and his weekends were often interrupted by the need to work overtime on a Saturday or Sunday.

He considered himself to have been "strangely isolated or insulated from humanity there." He was "encysted, so to speak, in the artists' colony, which is smug, quarrelsome and ingrown." He missed the basically human contacts and had "somehow repressed the knowledge of this need."[20]

Yet, apart from 1949-1952, which were rather sad, lean years, the remarkable fact of this period is his creative accomplishment. In 1955 Spud Johnson—writer, poet, former editor of *The Laughing Horse* (a famous little magazine of the 1920s in which D.H. Lawrence's work appeared) and close friend of Witter Bynner, D.H. Lawrence and Frieda Lawrence—wrote an article on Judson in his column *The Horsefly*:

> He's an amazing character who (quite apart from what he does and what he looks like—both of which are distinguished) should be a sort of model to all those Bohemian poets, painters, writers or artists who seem to think that "the world owes them a living," that they should be coddled and patronized and protected so that they can practice their art untrammeled by such sordid occupations as earning a

living, holding down a job, or bothering with the mediocre business of being a responsible citizen....

...Tremendous energy, channeled into an amazing capacity for work. After generally more than eight hours a day at his job as a printer and a presumed portion of his other waking hours devoted to his duties as a husband and father of two, he yet manages to run a rather unconventional bookshop, collect, edit, print or mimeograph several issues of a magazine (*Suck-Egg Mule* or *Deer and Dachshund*) and several volumes of verse (his own as well as the work of others) during the year—and, besides, to produce a sizable body of verse, which appears with frightening frequency in magazines all over the country.[21]

The Crews family lived in the old adobe house at Ranches of Taos for ten years, roughly 1950 to 1960. These were the years in which Carole and Anna Bush grew from infancy through childhood. It was a quiet rural environment. There were apricot and plum trees on the property. Each year Mildred cultivated a garden and the yard blossomed in myriad flowers under the touch of her green thumb.

Despite this isolation, they were witness to a coming and going of many people: artists, writers, poets, who came to Taos and to the home of Judson and Mildred Crews. It was a warm center in which they received friendship, hospitality and the most stimulating of conversation. Oftentimes it was shelter when they were in need. Mildred somehow managed to feed the unexpected guests, care for the girls, maintain the business of the home, and carry on her own creative photographic work. The miracle of feeding the multitude on a loaf of bread and a fish was accomplished—and the quality of the food and conversation was rich and palatable, sustenance for all who came.

Judson was bound to his job at the shop. Often, when there were guests and a party was under way, he would retire to bed early in order to be fit to carry on the next day.

The year 1960 marked another turning point. The Crews purchased a new home several miles closer to town, on the outskirts of Ranches of Taos, just off the highway near the Sagebrush Inn. It was a modern adobe home, formerly the residence of Buff and Kimball Blood, Taos artists. It had a remarkable vista of the mountain and the valley. Wide windows looked out over the desert, and the aspect of the mountains was austere.

The routine of labor at the newspaper office continued without respite. Changes in the editorial staff, changes in the ownership and publisher, seemed to make no difference to the status of Judson Crews. He continued working, the same long hours and for the same low wage, as a job printer.

Later Years

The break came in 1966. Anna Bush was ready to enter the University of New Mexico as a freshman. She had won a number of scholarships in high school, but they were not sufficient to cover the complete costs of education. Carole, the younger daughter, was to graduate from high school in June 1967. The time had come for a complete change.

He was unable to find work in the State of New Mexico as a social worker despite his M.A. With Honor in Sociology. It was a strange situation; many social workers were being hired who lacked even a B.A. degree.

Pursuing the matter further, he was interviewed by the Texas State Department of Welfare for a position at El Paso as a child welfare worker. He scored 103 points on the entrance examination and obtained the position, at a salary slightly lower than the one at the press in Taos. The family put the house up for sale and moved to El Paso in the summer of 1966.

They stayed in El Paso for a year, then moved to Wharton, Texas, about forty miles south of Houston. He had found a position on the staff of Wharton Junior College, where he began teaching sociology and psychology in September 1967.

He remained there until September 1969, when he resigned to take a job with the New Mexico Department of Hospitals and Institutions as a psychological counselor and representative of the New Mexico State Hospital in Gallup.

During the three years in Wharton Mildred had resumed her education, and she graduated with a Bachelor of Arts in Literature from the University of Houston in June 1969. They moved then to Albuquerque, where they rented a house until Judson could take up his position in Gallup in October.

In 1970 and 1971, while employed as counselor, he also taught part-time in the Sociology Department of the University of New Mexico Branch College in Gallup. Carole was married during this time to Ronald Jay Harrison in Austin, Texas. She graduated from the University of Texas in the summer of 1971 with a B.A. in art. She is a very talented young abstract painter, ceramist and print-maker.

Anna Bush Crews graduated from the University of New Mexico in June 1970, majoring in art and romance languages. She attended the University of New Mexico School of Modern Languages in Quito, Ecuador, during her junior year. Like her mother, she is an artistic photographer. In summer 1971 she applied to San Francisco State University, and was one of two students accepted for graduate work in the School of Photography. She received a Master of Arts degree in photography in the summer of 1973.

The years in Gallup were arduous. The community, set at the edge of the Navajo Reservation, a railroad and a U.S. 66 highway stop, represented isolation, culturally and socially. Judson's work was demanding, and he pursued it with characteristic energy, intelligence and dedication.

New Mexican politics under the reactionary administration of Governor Bruce King, together with the national climate of reactionary politics as represented by the Nixon Administration during its heyday with Agnew, Mitchell and Haldeman, did little to recognize the kind of service that a man like Judson Crews could offer. His dismissal from DHI was a loss to the State.

From his Gallup address he sought professional employment from October 1970 until October 1973. He continued teaching part-time at the UNM Branch College, and was a security guard for a private agency protecting the Gallup public schools and a company drilling for uranium at Church Rock. Mildred worked as a substitute teacher in the same school system.

Eventually he applied for a position as Director of the Intensive Care Unit at the State School for Girls in Chilicothe, Missouri. He made several trips to and from Missouri before securing the position. Mildred applied for a residency with the Wurlitzer Foundation in Taos, presenting as a project a book on the artists of Taos. She was successful, and moved into one of the Wurlitzer cottages in the summer of 1972.

Before leaving for Chilicothe, Judson stayed several weeks in November and December 1972 in a friend's cabin on the San Cristobal Valley Ranch above San Cristobal, writing poetry and answering much delayed correspondence. After spending the holidays with his wife and daughters in Taos, he left for Chillicothe to take up his new position in January 1973. Mildred remained at the Wurlitzer Cottage writing the book on Taos, and also writing much poetry herself, for the first time in many years. Her residency was renewed and she stayed in Taos until September 1973.

Judson worked in Chillicothe until August 1973. While there he applied for a teaching position in the Oppenheimer School of Social Work at the University of Zambia in Africa. His application accepted, he left Chillicothe and returned to New Mexico to await instructions from Zambia.

Meanwhile Mildred purchased an old adobe house on Talpa Ridge near Ranches of Taos. There was much work to be done on it, and Judson, with Anna Bush, who had returned from San Francisco, spent the next five months helping Mildred put it in order. After a long wait Judson and Anna Bush left Taos on January 11, 1974, to fly from Albuquerque to Lusaka, the capital of Zambia, via New York, London, Rome and Nairobi. They arrived in Lusaka on Monday, January 14, 1974. He was now 56; Anna Bush was 26.

In Lusaka they found housing in the University facilities. Anna Bush found a position at Evelyn Hone College in Lusaka, teaching journalistic photography and X-ray photography.

Judson's work at UNZA was very demanding of his time. In addition to lecturing, he was working in the field with his students. They were mostly Zambian, but some were from Nigeria, Tanzania, Rhodesia and other African nations. The faculty was cosmopolitan: European, American, Asian, African, South American, Australian and New Zealander. Africa at this time was in turmoil; revolution and anarchy were in the air.

He had little time for travel or other engagements. He did however frequent the streets of Lusaka, and produced a number of tapes of people talking. He transcribed and arranged from these tapes poems which were published in three books: *Voices from Africa*, which originally appeared in *Nexus* magazine in 1975; *Live Black Lusaka*, transcribed and arranged in Lusaka in 1974 and originally published in *Pembroke Magazine*; and *African Transcripts*, in *Obsidian*. Later, in the years 1978-1980, he republished the collections in three small chapbooks (4¼ by 7 inches) under the same titles: *Voices From Africa, Live Black Lusaka* and *African Transcripts*.

I have found a surprising parallel between Judson's methodology in transcribing and arranging poems from live voice tapes and that of the composer Béla Bartók, who produced musical compositions from the folk music of his native Hungary. Each has worked, in his own way as an artist, from the material he found in recording folk music and folk speech.

He also found time to write *Nations and Peoples*. This was a long revolutionary poem expressing the situation of the modern world and its turmoil, and especially the predicament of the third-world peoples. It would later be published in the United States by Cherry Valley Press in New York State, in *City Lights Anthology*, and by Buzzard's Roost Press in Las Cruces, New Mexico.

On recording the African street tapes, he wrote:

> I had applied for a Guggenheim, so I could at least hire an interpreter, and also a secretary. But I was turned down. So I was able to work only with an English speaking respondent....
>
> Of course, it is not the way people speak. But it is what they say, and it's their words. It is not meant as formal ethnology. I think it qualifies as poetry. And since the genius of African art, as Sekou Touré says, is anonymity, there are no name tags, and not even any tribal tags. I wasn't gathering statistics. All the respondents were Blacks....
>
> I finished up with less than fifty poems, never more than three or four from the same person, many I had to discard

completely. Now, I'm inclined to regret that I did not save some of the fragments to offer simply as fragments. But I was obsessed that poems could be made of the material. And in some cases it could not be. Though in some cases it was better than some of the things that were more complete. I'm glad I did it, but I am glad I am finished with it. I would not do it again, even if I could get a Guggenheim.[22]

It was during this African sojourn that he began working on his memoirs. They would take seven more years of work, in Africa, New Mexico and Baja California.

After four years he had fulfilled his contract with the University of Zambia. He was back in the United States by 1978.

Anna Bush went to Botswana and there taught photography to the personnel of the State Tourist Bureau. She traveled around Southwest and South Africa in a vintage Jaguar, taking many photographs of the country and its wildlife. She met a young man named Ian Wilson, a white African of Irish descent; they were married in London and have a son Sohrab. They have lived variously in Lilongwe (Malawi, Africa), in Qatar on the Persian Gulf, and in England. Anna Bush is now director of the F Stop Center in Bath, England, where classrooms and dark rooms are provided for photography students. She teaches classes and presents photographic shows.

Carole Crews later married John C. McLaughlin, a zoologist and writer who illustrates his own work. She lives in Ranches of Taos with their three children: Ariana, Edwina Claire and Iris.

Judson returned to the United States via Rome, Madrid and San Juan, Puerto Rico. It was the beginning of another period in his life of wandering, when he would domicile temporarily in Albuquerque, Ranches of Taos, Las Cruces and El Paso.

It was during this time that he and Mildred, after some thirty years of marriage, divorced by mutual consent. They were both artists working in their own ways. They had reared their children and were now free to concentrate upon their own work. Mildred had been a photographer for more than forty years and had begun to write. Over the years she has published many magazine articles, book reviews, accounts of the artists in Taos, short stories, and excerpts from a number of her novels. The two have remained friends and share a mutual interest in their daughters and grandchildren.

Judson then met Carol Bergé, a woman writer and university instructor of creative writing, with whom he had a rather tempestuous ten-year, on-and-off affair. During a three-year period (1978-1980) he published a large number of small poetry chapbooks of his own poems and those of several other poets, especially Carol Bergé, Emily F. Anderson and Wendell Anderson. Norman Moser called them "those little xerox fuckers." They were beautiful examples of small press publication operating on minimal means—"at a cost," said Judson, "considerably less than that of a cheap fifth of Scotch."

In 1980 he made a trip into Mexico with a young woman named Terry Taylor. They set out from El Paso in his little 1960 Volkswagen van for Baja California, where Terry was to study the care of goats. She was a nutritionist and very interested in the feeding and care of animals, as well as in the production of nutritious goat milk for cheese production. She and her former husband, Drew Wagnon, had once published a very good literary magazine, *Wild Dog*, out of Pocatello, Idaho. Later, she and Drew traveled the long route from the world of Haight-Ashbury in San Francisco to El Paso, where they established a small avant-garde bookshop on Mesa Avenue, directly in front of the University of Texas campus. Here at the *Chase Mansions Book Shop* Judson gave the first public reading of his poetry.

They arrived in Mulege, Baja California, after crossing the Sea of Cortés by ferry. There Terry took up her care of goats. Judson irrigated an orchard of tropical fruits in a high mountain canyon far from Mulege on one of the roughest roads in Baja California. He soon left to travel up the coast to Big Sur, and then cut back into the interior of California to visit one of his brothers in the Beaumont-Banning area.

At Big Sur he renewed his friendship with Emil White. He had returned to the locale of those war years when he had lived at Big Sur in close proximity to Henry Miller, which were the basis of a major part of the memoirs he had been writing for nearly seven years.

He made the circle complete by returning to New Mexico, where he eventually found residence in a public housing project in

Albuquerque. He also took up photography with a camera Anna Bush had given him.

There he has remained since, sending out his poems to the literary world, just as he has for more than fifty years. Young poets and writers have sought him out. They have communicated with him, contacted him by phone, and eventually visited him there, as did Gregory Smith:

> Poetry hasn't brought Judson Crews wealth or fame.... He is a humble man, as I learned during my several visits with him, and a generous man, in both his time and his work. There appears to be no bitterness in Judson Crews; he responds to queries about his successes and failures with an honest assessment of his own strengths and weaknesses. Though his health has been shaky in recent years, he remains fiercely independent, living alone, looking after himself, sharing company on a daily basis with his friend of almost fifty years, Wendell B. Anderson. Perhaps what I enjoy most about Judson Crews *the man* is that he has maintained a remarkable sense of humor, punctuating his great stories with loud laughter and raucous "well, goddamn!"s.[23]

He is representative now, not only of the present and the future, but of the immediate literary past of modern America. He is perhaps the best example of the poet who has created his own lifestyle and his own kind of poetry, without reference to either academia or the public market ruled by money and prestige. He is one of a kind, an original American poet of our time.

Notes

1. Letter to Wendell and Dodie Anderson, written from Camp Horn, Arizona, December 25, 1943.
2. Letter to Wendell and Dodie Anderson, written from Camp Adair, Oregon, July 11, 1943.

3. Full citations for all writings of Crews, and for critical material about him, may be found in the bibliography constituting the Appendix of this book.

4. Letter to Wendell and Dodie Anderson, written from Camp Adair, Oregon, July 18, 1943.

5. Letter to Judson Crews, written in 1973 when Judson was applying for the position in Zambia.

6. Beaudoin's memory of dates was fallible. Since the first issue of *Vers Libre* did not appear until 1936, the two men probably first met in the late 1930s.

7. Again Beaudoin erred; Crews and Tolbert were married in Taos in October 1947, two months before leaving for New York.

8. Letter to the author, July 21, 1968.

9. See "The Testimony of Henry Miller," Appendix of this book.

10. *The Brave Wild Coast.* (Submitted for publication.)

11. Letter to Wendell and Dodie Anderson, September 15, 1944. In 1946 Crews' Motive Press published a section of the thesis, "The Southern Temper," under that title.

12. *Big Sur and the Oranges of Hieronymus Bosch* (New York, New Directions, 1957), p. 12. The inaccuracies of this paragraph (Miller invited Judson to Big Sur many times, and they drank wine together on several occasions) are documented in the Appendix and text of *The Brave Wild Coast.*

13. Detailed descriptions of McKinney, Leite and many of the other artists and writers living on the Sur coast at the time are given in *The Brave Wild Coast.*

14. The first poems of Judson that Miller read (including "Casuals of War in a City that's Never been Bombed" and "Psalm for the Mortified Flesh") he called "fine" and "excellent." (Letters to Crews, August 10 and 30, 1944. Judson Crews papers, Box 3, folder 8.)

In 1944 Judson sent a copy of his thesis (see above, Note 11) to Miller, who was so impressed by "The Southern Temper" (see note 11 above) that he recommended it to James Laughlin of New Directions, and wrote to Crews: "It knocks blazes out of my book on America [*The Air-conditioned Nightmare*]. That's how I should have written mine!.... It's really a very moving thing, a poem, and white hot.... It made me dance inside.... You can write like the very devil." (Undated letter ["Saturday morning"], probably January 1945. Judson Crews papers, Box 3, folder 9.)

The Judson Crews papers may be consulted in the Special Collections Department, University Research Library, UCLA. Box 3, folders 8-10 contain 116 letters written by the Millers to Judson from 1942 to 1948: 96 from Henry and 20 from his wife Marta Lepska.

15. Letter to the author, written February 3, 1946 from Waco.

16. *Henry Miller: Full of Life*, p. 147, 222.

17. Miller's letter of January 18, 1944 (folder 8) is the most enthusiastic: "Whoever heard of a man collecting an author's work and then lending out sets to his friends? You are one out of a million."

18. Or one, if you prefer. Elliott Anderson and Mary Kinzie, in *The Little Magazine in America: a Documentary History* (Yonkers, N.Y., Pushcart Press, 1978), suggested that they could be considered one continuing magazine with different names and formats, dying and being reborn as Crews' personal finances waned and waxed. Three of them (*The Deer and Dachshund*, *Suck-egg Mule* and *The Naked Ear*) have come to be appreciated as classics of their genre. Of a high aesthetic as well as literary standard, they featured original works by such as William Carlos Williams, Robert Duncan, Robert Creeley, Langston Hughes, LeRoi Jones, Michael McClure, Diane Di Prima and Charles Bukowski.

19. *Henry Miller: Full of Life*, p. 230.

20. The quotations in this paragraph are from various letters of Crews to the author.

21. *El Crepusculo*, Taos, 1955.

22. Foreword to *Live Black Lusaka*.

23. *Atom Mind* 3(11):1, Summer 1993.

PART 2

The Poetry

SIX POEMS

The six poems analyzed in this chapter represent a certain integration. They were all written about the same time, which gives them not only a time context but a developmental context.

With the exception of "Stommer Bulltoven Crown," they were all written in a ten-month period in Taos. Interspersed was a five-month intermission in New York City, which produced only one or two tentative poems.

"What Babylon Was Built About"

Poem number 298 (the numbering is from Crews' card file) was written between May 9th and May 11th, 1948, a few days after returning to Taos from New York, and was first published in *Rough Weather*. Later it appeared in *Poetry*, and in the collections *The Wrath Wrenched Splendor of Love*, *To Wed Beneath the Sun* and *Come Curse to the Moon*.

> In this age of the machine
> must every line ring with mechanical precision
> the cool whir of the dynamo
>
> This is an age of the mind
> a mechanical mind stark in the face of dreams
> undone where consciousness recedes
> fear grasps where calculations fail
>
> Must I write a poetry of the mind
> of a stark mechanical mind

must red mean a reign of terror
black the gestapo hand

My mind is not a mechanical mind
my precision is only the heart's precision

Let them break their hard metaphors
on the sharp fragments I sew
let the dream trickle to the steel heart
and break its flow

Calculation has failed
no dream can flower in their frozen field
the mind is the jungle the heart gave birth in

The central motif of the poem is sounded in the first line, almost in the sense of Beethoven's opening bar of the Fifth Symphony: "In this age of the machine"...:

"Must every line ring with mechanical precision, the cool whir of the dynamo?" It is the poet asking of the time, asking of academia: must the line be institutionalized? Must the norm be only form, style, and a narrow, limiting precision?

"This is an age of the mind, a mechanical mind stark in the face of dreams, undone where consciousness recedes." Here the question is answered in part. We are living in an age of mental realization. When we lose our mechanical grasp and are faced with emotional reality, which demands an understanding of the totality of life—when we are faced with that which goes beyond our mental conscious mind, we are undone.

Finally the hard-driving point gathers added power, accumulative weight: "Fear grasps where calculations fail." We have come to the point where we depend solely on the cerebral processes for assurance.

Then the poet is again questioning: "Must I write a poetry of the mind, of a stark mechanical mind? Must red mean a reign of terror, black the Gestapo hand?" The reference is again to that which would confuse or limit the freedom of the pen to move within its appointed pattern of emotion giving form to the syntax. "Must red mean a reign of terror"? "Red" would under certain conditions—such as recent times, when red and communism were yoked together—mean just that; but the word "red" itself would freely connote many things, and "black" much other than the Gestapo hand.

The answer is given in the brief two-line fourth stanza. It is the credo by which the poet lives, the artistic ethos by which he lives and breathes. "My mind is not a mechanical mind; my precision is only the heart's precision." The poet rejects the world that would live only by the process of intellectualization without feeling, without a sense of the whole; the world that would only see the minute and would mistake a part for the whole. "Let them break their hard metaphors on the sharp fragments I sew; let the dream trickle to the steel heart, and break its flow."

Here is a comparison of the life force against the death force, the organic and the inorganic, fluidity and crystallization. "Let the dream trickle to the steel heart" asserts that the life force itself will break the steel heart of death. As, for example, in the Battle of Agincourt in *Henry V*, when a few thousand English yeomen, pitted against the armored horsemen of France and all the machinery of modern medieval warfare, defeated them by the application of a fundamental life principle: the massed fire power of leather-clad bowmen shooting upwards into the sun, the arrows dropping downwards into the faces of the knights. The men in armor, so heavy they had to be hoisted into the saddle by means of primitive cranes, once unseated from their saddles were helpless as broken robots on the ground.

"Let the dream trickle to the steel heart, and break its flow." The poem does not gamble. It only asserts a truth as old as life itself: that the life-force will always prevail over death, that there will be a return to the primal source, and the old crystallized, formalized institutions will in the long run fall.

In the last stanza: "Calculation has failed." Man and his calculation have floundered. Faith in the sense that we have known it in the past has left us. We have only our calculations, and all that the calculations have produced is the bomb.

"No dream can flower in their frozen field; the mind is the jungle the heart gave birth in." This itself coincides with the realizations of modern psychology. Regardless of the machinations of the obsessed and disturbed mind, deep down the basic emotions supply the main motive power of our acts.

The poem begins with the question, then informs us of the particular qualities of the age which demand "mechanical precision" of the
individual. It restates the question in stanza three, then begins to
answer it in two lines. The fifth stanza informs us that the attempt of
the mechanical forces to destroy life will fail. Then we find the dream
of the poet, his vision: the life force overthrowing the forces of death.
The last stanza presents a final answer to the original question.

The first person, "I," is the poet, the individual pitted against the
machine. It is the individual who would create the machine and destroy the machine and dream again, a better dream. Man's dream, out
of which come nightmares; but above, beyond, below and behind is
man, the dreamer and creator, in the beginning and in the end.

It is a poem of faith. It affirms again man's belief in man. Against
it the machines and "the mechanical mind"—"mammon," the mammon
of our age—are futile. The machine is impotent, but man is not.

The poem creates its own form as it flows or progresses. It is in free
verse, and divided into six stanzas. The first and last contain three
lines, stanza four has two, the remaining three have four each.

We observe the poet's art at work here. The division into these
peculiar stanzaic patterns is dictated by the needs of the poem itself.
The form of the work, as of all of Crews' poems, evolves in the creative free sense of William Carlos Williams' definition of the poem:

> A poem's movement is intrinsic, undulant, a physical
> more than a literary character....
> Each speech having its own character...the poetry it
> engenders will be peculiar to that speech, also to its own
> intrinsic form.
> When a poet makes a poem, mind you, he takes words
> as he finds them interrelated about him, and composes
> them without distortion which would mar their exact
> significances into an expression of his perceptions and
> ardour, that they may constitute a revelation in the
> speech which he uses.

What is significant in the form and structure of this poem is the
progression which happens to create the peculiar or distinct stanzaic

arrangement. As opposed to metrical, formal verse, where the form is arbitrarily imposed from the outset—a mold, as it were, into which the poem is poured—Crews' poems create their own form as they progress. "What Babylon Was Built About" moves simply from a question to an answer.

The first stanza carries no punctuation. There are neither question marks, commas, periods or semi-colons. They are not necessary; meaning lies within the arrangement of the line. It is within the diction and syntax that the poem carries its connotations.

How subtle in a sense is this rejection of the symbols of punctuation. It assists in cleaning up the poem. It assists in the "haiku sense" of meaning, in so far as *implication* of meaning (pointed up within the line itself) creates a question mark, a period, a comma. Only a poet of precision, utilizing an economy of words and lines, can carry a poem successfully in such a manner. It means a mastery, a command of the line itself.

Phrasal effectiveness is at work here. The poem proceeds in phrases: "in this the age of the machine"; "this is an age of the mind." A sentence will make up a stanza, beginning with the phrase for its line.

One of the qualities giving the poem unusual force and power is the skillful use of refrain or repetition. It does not intrude; instead it accompanies the thought of the poem almost like the pulse beat of the machine around which the thought of the poem evolves and revolves.

These rhythms of the machine are borne by the metronomic beat of such reiterated lines as "age of the machine," "age of the mind," "mechanical mind," "poetry of the mind," "the mind is a jungle."

Alliteration—as in the use of the letter M in "machine," "mechanical," "mind," "metaphor," or the letter C in "consciousness" and "calculation"— emphasizes and reinforces this progression and reiteration, while woven into the fabric of the poem.

The word "must" in stanzas one and three is repeated three times, not redundantly but in the refrainal sense, stressing the forces of compulsion at work on the individual in an age of the machine. Against this is a contrapuntal force in the answer implied, not stated, until we reach the fourth stanza: "My mind is not a mechanical mind; my precision is only the heart's precision."

The construction of the poem illustrates Williams' statement: "Each speech having its own character...the poetry it engenders will be peculiar to that speech in its own intrinsic form." At no point in the poem is there word intrusion which would mar this speech intrinsic to the form.

From the first beat, "In this the age of the machine," words such as "mechanical," "precision," "dynamo," "calculation" stress the abstract. Accompanying them are "fear," "red," "reign of terror," "gestapo." The controlling image of the poem is "the machine," the "mechanical mind"; in the symbolic sense it represents the forces of fear, compulsion, frustration and doubt.

The sleep-walking kind of death, accompanying the power of the machine, is brought forcefully to us by the cadence, the use of repetition, the variations played upon the theme in stanzas one, two and three.

It is difficult to speak of decorum in such a poem as this. The word choice with relation to the speaker, the occasion and the subject matter is particularly appropriate. It is beautifully controlled yet intense. It moves with the careful precision of the machine which it presents as the force to be dealt with.

"Bean Jack the Glore"

Poem 267 was written October 14th or 15th, 1947. It first appeared in *Three Hands*, and was republished in *The Anatomy of Proserpine* and *The Feel of Sun and Air Upon Her Body*.

> No wail it went the gladsome son
> he sought the wicked in the middle heart
> night was lonelier than a restless wing
>
> Wing the nettle his height was legerdemain
> meaning no heart
>   it shot the black ribbon
> ransom spoke through the waking snarl
>
> The handsome snake he was was a legend

Sailing was a legend
             alleged
                      fornicating
was a legend   O legendary heart   O heart
The sun brightened the poop deck as it rose

Rose was his name for her though christened Emily
rose because her body was so white
                          the ship of course
since he never loved another

His mother christened him John   this Jack

They rolled him in an old tarp   roped it good
the captain read a verse of scripture
and they heaved   him over
                  the swell
took him like an autumn leaf
Rose was his name for her   the poop deck bright

This poem moves with the music of a psalm. It is like an elegy, a ceremony at sea: the open sea with sun, the heaving deck and the body of the dead sailor being slowly dropped, draped, into the heaving waste. It is a eulogy to Bean Jack the Glore.

"No wail it went the gladsome son." The sailor is the gladsome son; no one regrets his departure.

"He sought the wicked in the middle heart; night was lonelier than a restless wing" acquaints us with the life of Bean Jack from the time he first put out to sea, a restless and lonely young man. If he had found any achievement in his career, it was in mischief: "His height was legerdemain...ransom spoke through the waking snarl."

He led the life of a typical sailor. If girls in port, if piracies, if smuggling were a part of the life, then so it was with Bean Jack. His glory lay in whatever adventure the life of the sea offered.

"The handsome snake he was was a legend." The devil was a legend more often regarded in the rough life of the sea, and seen perhaps more, than any other. For there were legends that inspired the young man, like others who went to sea: "Sailing was legend; Alleged fornicat-

ing was legend, O legendary heart, O heart." The yearning, the longing, the quest of the sailor....

Then the poem brings us back to the original scene, the ship and the
deck upon which the sea ceremony is being held—the burial of the
sailor, Bean Jack: "The sun brightened the poopdeck as it rose."

"Rose was his name for her though christened Emily; Rose because
her body was so white." This is a flashback, a reference to a sailor's
love. Then we are back to the sailor's life, to which he was bound:
"the ship of course, since he never loved another." Bean Jack in the last
resort had only the sea for his mistress and mother.

We are told that his mother christened him John. The sermon on
deck then proceeds: "They rolled him in an old tarp, roped it good; the
captain read a verse of scripture, and they heaved him over; the swell
took him like an autumn leaf." The rough ceremony at sea, the con-
finement of the roped body into the water, and the water's swell taking
it "like an autumn leaf" leave the reader gazing at the tableau on the
deck. The ship is there, like life moving on, "the poopdeck bright."

Logically the poem proceeds from "the gladsome son" who takes to
sea. His ransom for pursuing this life is described in twelve introductory lines. The concluding twelve lines bring us to the sea and the
ship. The final six present the burial at sea.

Its progression begins with the gladsome son: the Bean Jack, the
Jack tar. It proceeds from the sailor—"he sought the wicked in the
middle heart; night was lonelier than a restless wing"—to the sea:
"ransom spoke through the waking snarl." The idea here is both physical and psychological. "Waking snarl" is both the sea and the state of
mind.

The sea is suggested in the rhythms as well as named: "Sailing was
legend; alleged fornicating was legend; O legendary heart; O heart."
The intrusion of "the sun brightened the poopdeck as it rose" is a
vision, mystical. It is at this point that the very soul of the ship
emerges out of the sea, the symbol of Bean Jack's life.

We learn of his love, Rose. But she is a dual love: both Rose the
woman and Rose the ship. The next five lines reveal a lifetime. The
ship and the sea, Rose the sailor's sweetheart, the mother of the sailor,
and "John, this Jack."

It would seem superficially that the conclusion, the funeral of Bean Jack at sea, comes upon us without warning, but this is not the case. Throughout the poem we are informed by tense, the past tense: "night was lonelier," "the handsome snake he was was a legend," "sailing was a legend," "Rose was his name for her." The use of "was," the past tense in the verbals, strikes an elegiac note.

The first line, "No wail it went the gladsome son," sets the elegiac tone. A verb and an adjective—"Wail" and "gladsome"—connote here grief, or the lack of it, for the one who is lost. But the poem speaks of what was, who was, without allowing intrusion. We are not forced to accept the idea of a funeral at sea in the common elegiac sense. Thus the verse contributes to the sudden impact of the last six lines, when "they rolled him in an old tarp, roped it good."

The haunting sense which has been developed to this point is resolved, as if the sea's mist had opened and revealed the deck of the ship, the body roped in canvas, the Captain reading the Bible and the crew standing at attention. We return to grief: the poignant, sharp projection of grief suggested throughout the poem.

Nowhere, not even in Melville or Dana, shall we find a more moving picture of the sea than is reflected in the pathos of the sailor's life and love. The reiteration in the last line of the eulogy ("Rose was his name for her...") has a haunting poignancy.

The poem moves most musically. It represents a range of musical variation which can be expressed with the use of free verse in the hands of a skilled poet. The alliteration of the first line reads with the cadence of a saga. Along with the consonance and assonance, it tends to suggest something of the old Anglo-Saxon, as in *The Wanderer* and *The Sea Farer*. Also contributing to the flow of the poem is the extremely skillful use of the line employed with caesura, at certain points which simply in themselves serve as springboards into the unknown. This is the essence of true poetry.

It is a swift movement. Here and there a phrase interjected supplies the necessary meaning; the blank space and the picking up of the next line quickly carry the reader and the concept forward. The poem carries in its rhythms the suggestion of the heave and force of the sea: the long swells...the crashing of water...the smack of the waves against the prow of the lifting ship.

Its movement is undulant, becoming especially even-measured in "The sun brightened the poop deck as it rose." The elegiac mood is measured, as in a hymn: "They rolled him in an old tarp (the pause) roped it good" (the pause) "And they heaved him over (pause) the swell (pause) took him like an autumn leaf" (pause).

There is no need for extended clausal qualifications in such a poem. The phrase and its implications are sufficient to the reader. One reads as in a haiku sense such breaks as "The sun brightened the poopdeck as it rose /Rose was his name for her though christened Emily." Note how as the ship rose, the name Rose, his love, comes before us.

The use of the language and the intrinsic idea of the poem, the sea, are completely one. Mechanical structure and spirit are one. Night, the snake, ransom are symbols that reach out and become interwoven with the metaphor of the sailor's life. "Night was lonelier than a restless wing," "ransom spoke through the waking snarl," "the handsome snake he was was a legend": all characterize and qualify the nature of Bean Jack's pursuit and choice of trade.

The symbol of the ship is also the symbol of the sailor's love: "Rose was his name for her," "the sun brightened the poopdeck as it rose," "a verse of scripture." The reiteration is like a refrain: "Rose was his name for her (pause) the poopdeck (pause) bright." These are connotatively connected, and the double image is repeated in the final line of the poem.

The elegiac note is maintained throughout. The language of the sea pervades the poem: "Its night was lonelier than a restless wing." The mind associates it with the calm of the sea, of gulls. Words such as "legerdemain," "wicked," "ransom," "christened," the reference to the snake: all tend to lead us into the religious mystic aura which hovers around the poem.

"The Poise of Restless Wonder"

Poem 316 was written between May 17th and May 21st, 1948, and first published in *Poetry* about a year later. It was reprinted in *A Poet's Breath* and *To Wed Beneath the Sun*.

Oh but if he had coined a sin
                      no fame is like that
for he wracked his mind and grew pale
but the lasting dread was kind
                   it showered mercy
the winter and the wind was like that

He carried salt
               but tops and balls and twine
he had never organized his wonder
                       it left
before the flame was ripe, and the neighbor girl
he sinned with was never there

If the sun shone
          that was a wonder too if not a sin
for the earth was round and no God was needed
to make a ball
         even the snow would do that
granting the simple hill and the will of the wind
the birds came and went
              why not he

And when at last he grasped her hand
and she was quiet as the world stopped moving
and turned and ran
          the loom of hell
having seared his soul   no shame at all like that

"The Poise of Restless Wonder" is a psychological portrait.

"Oh but if he had coined a sin /no fame is like that." The protagonist craves masculinity. He wants to be dangerous, powerful: "no fame is like that."

"For he wracked his mind and grew pale /but the lasting dread was kind /it showered mercy /the winter and the wind was like that." He yearns for accomplishment. He would like to move the world, but these dreams are qualified by the realities of life and the difficulties of the time: "the winter and wind"—and, on second thought, his fears: "the lasting dread was kind...it showered mercy."

"He carried salt /but tops and balls and twine /he had never organized his wonder." His pockets are filled with a wondrous assortment of make-believe powers, "tops and balls and twine." He carries salt (truth), but "he had never organized his wonder." He had never been able to shape his dreams to the reality of himself and the world around him. "If the sun shone /that was a wonder too if not a sin /for the earth was round and no god was needed /to make a ball /even the snow would do that /granting the simple hill and the will of the wind /the birds came and went /why not he."

But, then, in his sense of freedom he tries his hand at life and at one of life's realities, a first love. And when at last he grasped the neighbor girl's hand, "and she was quiet as the world stopped moving /and turned and ran /the loom of hell /having seared his soul; no shame at all like that."

It is here that he fails to rise above the original sense of guilt. He wanted to sin. He dreamed of sinning (for there was no fame like that). He wanted to be alive and vivid with life, but he could not. "He had never organized his wonder."

The poem tells of the damage wrought upon the individual by over-idealization, over-intellectualization. Reality and the facts of life do not coincide with the individual's capacity to realize and fulfill what he is. Because of his sense of guilt he could not sin as he wished he could. It was "the loom of hell having seared his soul."

Thus it is a poem of the state of perpetual unbeing realized by countless individuals. It is a poem about the frustration of the soul, about the doom of the individual institutionalized by his psychological problems. We have Hamlets such as this by the million and Miniver Cheevys uncountable in today's atomic world.

The meaning of the poem goes far beyond a personalized dilemma. It reaches into psychological meanings having to do with environment, childhood and social forces, as presented in the compulsion of religious dogma.

Here such words as "dread," "mercy" and particularly "sin," repeated in each of the first three stanzas, impress upon the reader the force of the concept as it shapes his life.

"The neighbor girl" is a key figure. She represents the possible liberating force by which the protagonist could lift himself from his dilemma of sin and guilt. But she is not enough.

The particular poignancy of the poem lies in the frustration of this will-to-woman which is the will-to-life. "Oh but if he had coined a sin; no fame is like that."

The dilemma is stated; the resolution, foregone, is forebodingly suggested by "but the lasting dread was kind."

The protagonist's attempt to break from his tightly bound world of fear and doubt are at every point frustrated. The drama of the poem revolves within this squirrel-cage dilemma: "He had never organized his wonder."

The invocation to nature in the third stanza finds the protagonist frustrated even here. "The birds came and went; why not he?"

Shame and guilt, the sense of sin, are the elements shaping his orientation to life. The implication of the poem is that the powerful emotional force of inhibition is more than can be managed by the hero. He is defeated even before he begins by the forces that have shaped him. All attempts to escape, particularly by means of willing or by rationalizations, are nothing compared to the power of inhibition, subconsciously seated. "For he wracked his mind and grew pale, but the lasting dread was kind."

The hero is unable to mentally wrest himself from his dilemma. He is confused: "He carried salt, but tops and balls and twine": these are symbols of boyhood. "He had never organized his wonder"— that is, he had never matured beyond this boyhood state. This sense of wonder too has departed: "It left before the flame was ripe."

In the final dénouement ("and when at last he grasped her hand, and she was quiet as the world stopped moving"), he turns and runs. "The loom of hell having seared his soul, no shame at all like that."

The poem is written in cadenced free verse, in four stanzas. The first two contain six lines each; the third, eight lines; and the last, four. The form is determined by the needs of the poem, and is created out of its intrinsic need and movement. Tension is built up; the poem evolves within a formal frame like a Bach fugue.

It is an account of an individual dilemma, and the point of view is expressed in the third person, "he." The first stanza introduces the protagonist: "Oh but if he had coined a sin." The second progresses to the reason for his quandary, his lack of organization, "the neighbor girl he had sinned with." In the third we find an elucidation of his reason for not feeling guilt. The fourth stanza presents us with the irrefutable fact of his dilemma: he cannot resolve himself, he cannot exorcise his sense of guilt.

"No Father Where the Light is Shed"

Poem 257 was written on October 10th or 11th, 1947. It was first published in *Rough Weather*, and reprinted in *Come Curse to the Moon* and *Inwade to Briney Garth*.

> The whip was broken because it was old
> it was predicated as a metaphor
>
> No metaphor has bitten the wind
> with such sharp teeth
>
> No metaphor has lain in wait
> so many hours
>
> My eye is like a second nostril
> no winter has blinded it
>
> Caution was written into my countenance
> because the seasons were treacherous

I would break all metaphors
across the bared nates

No mind should gobble the dung
the heart excretes

This complex, enigmatic poem is a metaphor on the metaphor. It warns us of the trap into which metaphor may lead.

"The whip was broken because it was old; it was predicated as a metaphor. No metaphor has bitten the wind with such sharp teeth." The whip is the old law. While the law was effective, its metaphor was applicable and strong to its central vision.

"No metaphor has lain in wait so many hours." But metaphors that have lain in wait for so long threaten to cloud our insights, and are brought up short. The poet refuses to be led into this labyrinth: "My eye is like a second nostril; no winter has blinded it."

Regardless of the winter of the seasons, the disturbances of the time, he is cautious. "Caution was written into my countenance because the seasons were treacherous." Despite the law and the metaphor pertinent to it, the poet has not been lulled, has not been blinded to the reality, the truth. In this time of many passing fashions—in thought, politics, in every phase of human endeavor—the poet is listening to another beat. Because the times are treacherous, because treachery and betrayal have become a common occurrence, he must be cautious.

"I would break all metaphors across the bared nates." All metaphors are the result of cerebral peregrinations. They become in time only red herrings cast across the trail of our perception of reality. By means of the long extended metaphor, the original truth is lost, dogma and institutions arise and bury it. Thus the poet would break them all.

"No mind should gobble the dung the heart excretes." The heart will, yes, yield up metaphor upon metaphor, in its anguish and confusion, the more so when the mind is confused—for analysis will suggest analogy *ad infinitum* even though the center be gone. But we should not take the endless unwinding of metaphors for the law of an original truth. Any unwinding of metaphors from the truth is in time bound to be absurd.

Even the title, "No Father Where the Light is Shed," is a metaphorical reference; it is in itself the symbol of the poem. The father is authority. Light is a reference to understanding. In one sense the title, like a haiku, is a microcosm of the entire poem, which becomes an elaboration of the symbol projected.

The poem itself begins and ends with metaphors. In the first words, the whip again describes the law, the Father. In the last, "the dung the heart excretes" is the betrayal of truth by metaphor.

The seasonal reference is a frequent symbol in the poetry of Crews. Winter is the time of crystallization, a season of death. In the next line ("the seasons were treacherous") the term is used to convey the element of unpredictability. On a larger scale it refers to the day, the age, the political clime in which we live. These seasons are treacherous and would betray us or lead us astray, as we are led astray by metaphors no longer connected to an original significance.

In such a way we may refer to the metaphor of political events and the evolution in the minds of people led astray by a public image, which is in itself only a metaphor in the mind. Sometimes a public image will resolve itself in the public mind to such an extent that only the metaphor persists and the meaning and the being have evaporated. The public mind thus mixed with metaphor seems to consist only of endless metaphors of meaning as exemplified in the public figure, popularly chosen. Each evocation of the public image only reinforces the metaphor and causes it to be swallowed again and again.

The poem is written in seven two-line stanzas in free cadence form. It is an excellent example of the realization of form without rhyme or meter; of form taking place and finding place within the orbit of the emotion that creates it. It is also an excellent example of William Carlos Williams' dictum: "A poem is perfect machine, no one word is irrelevant or redundant, all parts work perfectly and completely together."

The rhythm is measured, concise. There is a chipped emphatic quality to the way the lines are phrased: "The whip was broken because it was old /it was predicated as a metaphor." Then the thought is taken up quickly, succinctly: "No metaphor has bitten the wind /with such sharp teeth." Then the reiteration, strong, reaffirming the thought: "No metaphor has lain in wait /so many hours." The phrases follow, one from the other, weaving in and out.

The lines are packed with an abbreviated intensity of meaning. The unity is extremely direct, clear—almost bald. Stripped, as it were, of the content that would make for misleading metaphor. In one sense, aphoristic. In another, more purely imagistic.

Each line is in itself a phrase so arranged that it is a springboard to the next, and the connotation and allusion reaching out from the poems is like a stone striking water, leaving concentric circles ever-widening outwards.

Again we have the creation of a form out of the context of the poem itself. However it emerges, it is this form—self-contained, within the particular speech issuing from the perceptions and feeling—that, as Williams says, "constitutes a revelation in speech."

"Stommer Bulltoven Crown"

Poem 323 was written between April 5th and 23th, 1953, and appeared the same year in *Accent*. It is one of the poems that relate to "Bean Jack the Glore," a number of which appeared together in his collection *The Anatomy of Proserpine*, a long, unfinished poem. "Stommer Bulltoven Crown" may also be found in *The Heart in Naked Hunger* and *To Wed Beneath the Sun*.

> Stommer hell loose woeing the sun
> this canticle was meant for you
> scoffer though you may have been
> pussy baiter though you surely were
>
> The war exerted an evil eye
> though the year was shot
> before it began
>   chagrin was our molten crown
> cringing no vice in our full agenda.

Lindamyra playing you for a full fool
rum full though you surely were

and then Bulltoven
            Bully Mac Bulltoven
cursing against the sky
cursing the bridge, the bow
his bloody bones no doubt
are cursing still

But you, Stommer, hell loose as I have said
hell loose but woeing
the naked sun

It seems almost as if Crews' sea pieces were memories of another
life lived, in another world, in another time. Were I a Buddhist, or
were the poet, I would say that we were reading a work of the creative
imagination.

This poem opens with a presentation of Stommer: "Stommer hell
loose woeing the sun, this canticle was meant for you" presents the
protagonist, an image certainly of a swashbuckler, a male, a vigorous,
passionate being. We learn that he was a scoffer, and a pussy baiter. He
might be then a character akin to Lars in Jack London's *The Sea Wolf*.
He likes women and strong drink as only a man of the sea would. The
depth of his ability to feel, to sense, is revealed in the fact that he was
a scoffer--"hell loose woeing the sun"--he woes the sun of being.

In the second stanza we are identified with Stommer in the situation
of a world at war. "The war exerted an evil eye, though the year was
shot before it began; chagrin was our molten crown, cringing no vice
in our full agenda." The predicament of man is the betrayal of the man-
to-man relationship. This is embarrassing to Stommer, and in the
symbolic sense embarrassing to man.

We wear a crown, which represents our cringing before this predicament. Our wearing it also indicates that as men we assume the
responsibility of our consciousness, painful as it may be. It is no
wonder that Bulltoven woes the sun of our being, of his being.

The Lindamyra of the fourth stanza informs us of one of the reasons
for Stommer's dilemma, a woman with whom he is involved. He has

been played for a fool by Lindamyra. He takes the seaman's grog: "rum full." He will insulate himself from this predicament to bear it as well as he can.

Another figure is presented in the next stanza, Bully Mac Bulltoven, who, caught in this predicament, was unable to do anything but curse and die: "cursing against the sky, cursing the bridge, the bow, his bloody bones no doubt are cursing still." Stommer, and the rest of us, are placed with Bully Mac Bulltoven in this dilemma, this tragedy of war.

The final stanza returns to Stommer, to the irreconcilable position of a man who is "hell loose but woeing the naked sun."

Stommer is struggling to achieve a sense of manhood against one of failure and frustration. The crown is the crown of man's sense of being. Stommer woes the naked sun from which he cringes; he cringes from the naked act of man living in pure assertion of self as man. It is a sense of manhood such as we have not known in our time—but the image of a man which we all, in our own soul, know to be true. The molten crown of this consciousness burns when it seems as if there is no way to stand up again as men. We are only parts of a mass of men engaged in the murder of men. "Cringing no vice in our full agenda" refers to the fact that man has no ground but violence to stand upon and, being forced to accede to these conditions, cringes. Cringing is not the vice it would generally be, in the full agenda of the vices attendant to the total ends of total war.

Our calculations cannot awaken us to a sense of being. We merely register fragmentary glimpses of what manhood can be. We have a presentiment of man's being as it was, perhaps, in the old heroic sense of the Greeks.

Stommer's protest is viewed sympathetically. We are somehow identified with him and his dilemma. His solution—"hell loose"—engages our active sympathy. His frustration symbolizes our collective frustration at forces operating beyond our control.

The power of the poem lies in the evocation of this emotion, a commingling of rage, frustration and conviction. No matter if Bully Mac Bulltoven dies at the bridge of a torpedoed ship, or Stommer drinks and curses. We are assured by the emotional message that these feelings are justified.

The poem provides no answer, no resolution of the dilemma other than that of feeling. We learned in "What Babylon Was Built About": "Calculation has failed. No dream can flower in their frozen field; the mind is the jungle the heart gave birth in." It is a matter of the heart's anger.

The crown of the title has its referent within the poem: "chagrin was our molten crown." We wear the burning crown of the knowledge of our frustration: our impotence, as men, in this collective madness, this dilemma. The protagonist's pain is the pain of all men of sensibility. It is the burning hot crown that sits on the brow of the soul. These men, Stommer and Bully Mac Bulltoven, symbolize it for us. They wear it for us...burning red hot upon the brow...molten.

The sun is a central symbol, a symbol of freedom, strength. In the first line Stommer "woes the sun," and the poem ends: "hell loose but woeing the naked sun." The right to live in the sun as man under the sun is denied. We find the reiteration of Bulltoven's frustration in such words as "chagrin," "cringing," "woeing" and in the cursing of Bully Mac Bulltoven.

The poem is a non-metrical hymn or song addressed to Stommer. Five stanzas mark its form, arranged in four, five, two, six and three lines. The phrasal quality dominates, as it does in almost all of Crews' poetry. Note how the fugues weave in and out, again a Bachian structure. The speech is almost clipped, concise, yet most informative without redundancy.

The assonance lends much to the cadence and musical ring: "Stommer," "woeing," "sun," "scoffer," "pussy baiter," "surely," "were." There are musical alliterations, such as "molten crown cringing," which carry the technical poetic structure to completion as diction.

Repetition, used sparingly but effectively, reinforces certain passages at the right moment: "cursing against the sky, cursing the bridge, the bow"; "scoffer though you may have been, pussy baiter though you surely were."

The diction is most appropriate to the subject matter, and achieves the sympathy or empathy of the canticle. "Bloody," "cursing," "woe," "fool," "scoffer," "evil," contribute effectively to the tone of the poem's lament. A song in which only our sympathies can be evoked, and in a manner similar to Bulltoven and Stommer, we can only curse and beat our fists upon the closed door of the collective madness of war.

"Delve In the Secret Mind"

Poem 80 was written on October 10th or 11th, 1947. It was first published in *Simbolica*, then collected in *Come Curse to the Moon* and *The Feel of Sun and Air Upon Her Body.*

Love in abstract is like mechanics of space
being fold in fold upon fold
the dimension in a power of "n"
The astronomer himself nebulous
                                        nebuli
the subject of his deep devotion
the subject of his deep dread
                                the inverse number
calculated from a mobile point
on an imaginary ellipse transverse to the sun

night and day are one
each being several quadrillions but each
divided by infinite hours

This time is the time of love
                                in abstract
the day of simpler law is set aside
This is the day of mechanistic space
when even nothing has volume and motion
but love is less than these
                        an abstraction

of disintegrated sun never viewed   never charted
rumored only
                once to have been imagined.

"Love in abstract is like mechanics in space." The mechanics in space refer to the theories of astronomy. The mechanics are said to be "fold in fold upon fold." They are "the dimension in the power of n," a theoretical unwinding *ad infinitum.*

The motif of definition is sounded here in the first three lines. Already the attempt to define "love" is comparable to the attempt to define space and infinity.

"The astronomer himself nebulous nebuli, the subject of his deep devotion, the subject of his deep dread." The astronomer, observing and studying the stars, realizes the infinite and man's minute presence among them. He is like a priest devoted to the study of the heavens. Yet, observing and studying, he is "filled with dread," the dread of the realization of his smallness. Thus the astronomer calculates "from mobile point." He must make "an imaginary ellipse transverse to the sun."

The next stanza recapitulates the motif sounded in the beginning, that of futility, of abstraction and idle speculation. The calculation of infinity reveals that "night and day are one, each being several quadrillions but each divided by infinite hours."

Then the third stanza: "This time is the time of love, is abstract; the day of simpler law is set aside." Man cannot love as long as he attempts to realize love through abstraction—the idea of love compared to its simpler, basic, human matrix of feeling, passion, of meaning without cerebral *knowing.* "The day of simpler law is set aside."

In short, man has become complex and separate from his sources by his endless, minute calculations. He has plucked the petals of the rose and there is no rose left.

Reference is made to the sciences and the technology of our time: "This is the day of mechanistic space, when even nothing has volume and motion," and the poem concludes: "but love is less than these, an abstraction of disintegrated sun never viewed, never charted, rumored only once to have been imagined."

In this conclusion we have the summation of the idea of the poem, the central image that love and the power to love have been lost because of our tendency to abstract, intellectualize. We have wandered astray. We are benighted.

The key metaphor of the poem is "astronomer." This figure-abstracted, studying nebulas through a telescope—is like ourselves in our removal from life. We have removed ourselves from love by our speculations, our mental conceptions of love. Such terms as "dimension in power of n," "quadrillions," "mechanistic space," "the disintegrated sun," all operate with images of science, abstraction, intellectualization.

This alienation can be multiplied by the manifold abstractions defining the culture: the T.V. watcher, the automobile (insulating travelers across the city and through the countryside), the vicarious "sit in" spectacles of sports, politics, entertainment, and of history in the making.

"Disintegrated sun" connotes to our mind the atom, nuclear fission, and that paean to the perfidy of man, the atomic bomb. Here is one indubitable result of our nose-to-the-line speculations. The poem both connotes and denotes this perception: how intellect in the absence of emotional realization leads, in the present instance, from Marie Curie's discovery of radium to the final Manhattan Project in which a whole corps of scientists feverishly worked towards the fiendish result.

Here, too, is a description of impotence: "but love is less than these, an abstraction of disintegrated sun never viewed, never charted, rumored only once to have been imagined."

"Night and day are one, each being several quadrillions but each divided by infinite hours" reflects a truth symbolized by one of the great psychoanalysts, Wilhelm Stekel, who said, "Time is the money of love."

Modern man thus is likened to the astronomer surveying a universe without end, for love abstracted as such becomes a universe not only unreachable but unrealizable, before which the nebulous astronomer, Man, watches—"the subject of his deep devotion, the subject of his deep dread" never arriving.

Here again movement and meaning create the form. A free-verse cadenced form, as symmetrical as anything found in metered verse.

The opening line, "Love in abstract is like mechanics in space," is followed by two lines qualifying "love" and "abstraction." Then the poet projects the scientific image of space and science. The image is developed of the astronomer, who is also a symbol.

The third stanza is concerned with time: mechanical, chronological, scientific. In the fourth, "the time of love" is contrasted with "abstract time" of science. The fifth and final stanza, as in a sonnet, drives home the abstract comment. It resolves the proposition set forth in line one.

The feeling of the poem is skillfully woven with the music of its assonance: "abstract," "mechanics," "space," "astronomer," "nebulous," "subject," "devotion," "inverse," "number."

Significant is the exclusive quality of the diction. It is a poem of the modern world, of science. Its form has created, according to Williams' definition, "A small or large machine made of words." The theme of abstraction is revealed in the terminology of abstraction, mathematics, science: "dimension," "power of n," "nebulous," "inverse number," "calculated," "ellipses," "transverse," "law," "mechanistic," "volume and motion," "disintegrated."

The character of this speech has given it its intrinsic form, its meaning pervading, enriching it with its power. Its beauty is achieved by its symmetry. A convolution, sinuous with itself.

Microcosmically the poem is a picture of the whorls of the cerebrum, the convolutions of the brain. Read it from any point of view; its integrity of form and content is complete.

It moves in measured cadence. Its decorum is admirably suited to the subject. An almost metronomic count in cadence is utilized, each impinging upon the ear. One thinks of sonar or of radio telescope, or of machines registering the convolutions of the brain in sleep. Only here it is the sensitive poet registering the mind and mood of modern man.

CREWS ON POETRY

It would be difficult to hold Judson Crews down to some narrow definition of the meaning of poetry or the meaning of art, and to ask him what particular form it should follow. But over the years he has made several statements on these matters, in articles, reviews, and letters; by examining them we should at least catch an idea of some of the main sources or points of reference, his basic ideas and beliefs.

First, on his beginnings:

My own poetry is in no sense exemplary. The few good poems I have written have been essentially spontaneous. I started out at twenty, after a three or four years' false start, with very loose but conventional rhymed forms, with a clean, imagistic poem. For some fifteen years I sloshed knee, arms, and waist deep in "Gongorism." For several years now I have been writing clean poems in what I imagine to be Williams' "American idiom" sense.

I wrote short stories and poetry throughout my college years, taking what writing courses I was able to get, including a play-writing course taught by Lynn Riggs. I won several campus literary awards though my winning stories "couldn't be published." One was published by Ray B. West in his *Rocky Mountain Review* and two or three others in other off-campus publications. Poetry appeared in *Bozart-Westminster*, *Iconograph* and elsewhere.

I was unable to write in the Army (World War II), and when I returned to the university I was too busy with my thesis (M. A.) to do any creative writing. Henry Miller said of the Faulkner sections of my thesis that this was the way one writer should write of another.

I returned to my poetry writing while at Big Sur in 1945, though still working in a primarily imagistic mode. The poetry particularly represented a kind of breakthrough to a more "metaphysical dimension." Both of these pieces of work were so badly reviewed, however, that I decided to stop writing altogether. I returned to the university in September, 1946, to study art.

In the meantime Dorothy Norman accepted a group of these poems for *Twice a Year* and Caresse Crosby accepted a group for *Portfolio*. However, both magazines discontinued publication before the work was used. Later, after I learned printing, I printed up the "best half" of the book myself as a pamphlet.

I moved to Taos in June 1947 to continue my art studies but spent more time writing poetry than painting. During the next eighteen months I produced a respectable portion of some of the best poetry I have ever written. Hayden Carruth later accepted a group of these for *Poetry Magazine*, which under the editorship of Karl Shapiro continued to be one of the few established magazines which would occasionally publish a sampling of my work.

Since 1948 I have been able to write sporadically on occasional weekends. None-the-less I continue to produce a considerable body of work and I continue to make advances in it, especially, I think, during the last four or five years.

During 1963 and 1964 I had finished 97 poems; 32 of these have been accepted for publication in *Poetry*, *Wormwood Review*, *Per Se*, *Simbolica*, and other magazines. I have also produced a similar number of poems during this period which for one reason or another I still consider unfinished.

I have never known how to make contacts in the publishing world and derive virtually no general recognition and no income from my writing.[1]

On the academic world and the role of the poet, he continues:

Unduly impressed by the unfortunate records of Yvor Winters, John Crowe Ransom, and Paul Engle in the role of poet as professor, I made a hasty exit from Academia at the age of thirty knowing that teaching would warp the poet's view of the world and dry up his soul.

Reconsidering the question more recently on the basis of the records of Charles Olson, Robert Creeley, and Edward Dorn, I must concede that after all it may constitute a marriage of true minds. The earlier poets in the position of poet-professor may have died on the stem even if they had chosen to be "hod-carriers."

In short the boogey-boo of Academicism has been largely misunderstood or misstated. An education, even a continuing education, can only be serviceable to the poet. The comparative affluence, however, and the temptation to divert one's talents (grants, fellowships, editorial tid-bits) associated with bourgeois status is likely to be confused with the way of virtue itself (*vide* John Ciardi and the late Theodore Roethke).

The poet must remain the "Rebel" in Camus' exemplary sense of the word. In this respect, the academic setting may offer a danger to the conformist and the academic stooges, but for the real poet it may also offer an opportunity.

In some respects I regret that I passed up this opportunity or allowed it to pass me up. However, student magazines, edited by students and read by students, are still the most ready source of publication for my work. So possibly this default on my part is more imaginary than real.[1]

Elsewhere he sums up his views:

The threat of "Academicism" is hardly as great as some envision it. Some are strangled by the umbilicus in the womb, but for most it is a life-giving cord. When fully born you cut it off.

But the scar is not as unsightly as all of that. Pound and Williams and H.D. all wrote sonnets together at college. Only a fool would say it did *them* much harm.[2]

The following passage from a letter of 1966 refer to the struggle the poet had during the long years in Taos when he was working as a job-printer. It also illustrates his belief in the role of the poet.

Poetry is my vocation, and in spite of long years of heavy physical labor and a social climate [Taos] hostile to all things literary or intellectual, I have continued to produce and publish at a level considerably higher than most would expect.

However, my critical writing has suffered. I can write a poem, quite literally, standing on a street corner, but to write even a book review will require the major portion of my lunch hour over a period of two or three weeks.[3]

From another letter:

My vocation is poetry, but if I ever lived in an ivory tower at all, it was certainly for very brief periods of time. However, during my more than fifteen years in Taos, I was strangely isolated or insulated from humanity, encysted, so to speak, in the artists' colony there which is smug, quarrelsome, ingrown. I am absolutely certain that my decision to move out again into the stream of humanity is one of the best decisions I have ever made in my life. How I missed the basically human contacts; but how I somehow suppressed the knowledge of this need.[4]

Finally:

"Bourgeoisism" is the greater danger. Roethke applied the term "bourgeois" to Shapiro, so Shapiro applies it to himself. It would at least be as applicable for Ginsberg (whom I none-the-less personally like). A bathtub will not make you bourgeois, but press notices will. A hi-fi set will not make you bourgeois, but penthouse parties might. The artist must be a "rebel" in Camus' exemplary sense of the word, and pot, inversion, or Zen can have very little to do with it.[2]

In 1952 Crews published a review of William Carlos Williams' autobiography. Extracts suggest his approach to poetry:

Most of the reviewers seemed shocked, and several deeply offended, at Williams' characterizing the appearance of T.S.

Eliot's *The Waste Land* as "the great catastrophe to our letters ...which gave the poem back to the academics." This,
however, is the key to the importance of what he has stood
for as a man and as an artist.

That T.S. Eliot broke the back of the New Poetry movement in America goes without question. That W.H. Auden
delivered a second staggering blow is equally self-evident.
John Gould Fletcher recognized this and published an article
on the subject in the early '40s. He was less well equipped
than Williams, however, to make a living example against
academicism in his own poetry.

This is Williams' importance to contemporary letters,
that he has been steadfast to the ideal of non-academicism.
It is for this reason that a knowledge of Williams' work is
important to any beginning writer today. The university
quarterlies, generally, are committed to academicism. This is
why the little magazine is still important and still necessary
and why Williams has been its constant friend and
champion.[5]

The second portion of the same article is a review of *An Examination of Ezra Pound* by Peter Russell.

That he [Ezra Pound] has been widely attacked I know very
well. As early as 1914, Eunice Tietjens, writing in *The Little
Review*, in an attack on *vers libre* stated that to see the
tendencies which she had described in their "most exag-
gerated form" it was necessary to go to the work of Ezra
Pound. However, she appended, to attempt to lay the entire
onus of "so flagrant a spiritual and cerebral degeneration" to
the writer of free verse was not possible.[5]

Here we find a warm appreciation of what Pound was and means
as a poet and a literary force. He continues:

However, Pound is known as *The Poet*, not as a human
being. He himself has contributed much to this myth....
Pound is *The Poet*. America hates poets, and they have con-

sistently attacked and vilified Pound. That he is anti-Semitic, that he is a traitor, that he is "high priest" of the "New Criticism," are only excuses current. Actually the attacks on Pound are attacks on Poetry. The protestations of the attackers that they are defending poetry is added substantiation of this view.[5]

A comparison of the poet's concepts and beliefs, in the light of his own statements and as reflected in his poetry, reveals a remarkable correlation between statement and fact, ideal and act.

His conception of *vers libre* itself has been exemplified in his editorial stance throughout the time that he was editing *Motive, Suck-Egg Mule, The Naked Ear, The Deer and Dachshund, Poetry Taos* and *Taos: A Deluxe Magazine of the Arts*. He has never claimed that the poetry he published was better than others'. He simply selected the literature of which he personally approved.

Crews' diversity and versatility of range in poetic experimentation attests to a steady growth from one phase to the next. He is capable of close examination without falling into subjectivity. His mind is open. He is able to extend a viewpoint beyond that previously held when experience or reality suggests a change. Yet the change is registered without a loss of the essential center of balance which is his being. He examined the validity of "Academia" itself, and when the time came he was able to perceive the way and go forward without sacrificing his essential belief and faith in himself. "The poet must remain the 'Rebel' in Camus' exemplary sense" represents this center.

Finally, Crews has always been an advocate and champion of the rights of free speech—a concern not only fundamental to all men and women but of particular concern to the writer.

He has not only editorialized and written articles on freedom of speech; he has represented his viewpoints in person, in discussions of such matters as the censorship of films in the Taos community. *The Dorian Book Quarterly*, commenting on his efforts to preserve "the rights of free speech" in America said: "He calls the hand of the censors."[6] It reprinted two of his letters from the local *Taos News* in which he had in unequivocal terms pointed out the illegality of censorship, presenting the constitutional facts as embodied in the freedom of press guarantee in the First and Fourteenth Amendments to the United States Constitution.

Spud Johnson printed his article, "The Anatomy of the Censor," in *The Horsefly*. Reviewing *Book Selection and Censorship* by Marjorie Fisk,[7] Crews wrote:

> The purpose of books is to record both the wisdom *and* the folly of mankind. The purpose of education is to understand *both* of these elements in human experience.
>
> The First Amendment to the Constitution states quite bluntly that "Congress shall make no law...abridging the freedom of speech or of the press."[8]

Four basic facts emerged from this review: "The censor is against sex," "The censor works outside the law," "The censor seldom reads," and "The censor represents a minority." He insisted that

> The censor is narrow, bigoted and ignorant. He always represents a very, very small minority in any community; but because he is aggressive, arrogant and over-riding, he will generally represent himself as speaking for various organizations: generally church and school groups, but sometimes civic organizations as well. Local officials rarely have either the integrity or the interest to stand up against the demands of the censor.
>
> Librarians, particularly in tax-supported libraries, are very vulnerable to repressive tendencies from within the community. But there is one big factor in their favor. It is not very difficult to combat ignorance with knowledge. If and when literate people become aware that the stupidest element of the community is setting the standard for what they can or cannot read, the battle for the Freedom to Read is already well on its way to being won.[8]

Crews' dedication to his vocation, poetry, and to all of the techniques, ideals, beliefs and rights connected with the art, are attested by the quality of his poetry and the nature of his being as a man.

Notes

1. Letter to E.V. Griffith, editor of *The Hearse*, ca. 1967.
2. Letter to the author, ca. July 1968.
3. Letter to Alan Sawey, Head, Department of Communications, Pan American University, Edinburg, Texas, May 14, 1966.
4. Letter to Ernst Borenski, Chairman, Social Science Division, Tougaloo College, Mississippi, June 26, 1966.
5. *Suck-egg Mule*, #5.
6. *Dorian book quarterly,* 4th quarter 1960.
7. Berkeley, University of California Press, 1959.
8. *The Horsefly*, June 9, 1960.

THE RECEPTION

Criticism[1]

Beaudoin

Crews' first collection of poetry, *Psalms for a Late Season*, a pamphlet, was published in 1942 by Kenneth Lawrence Beaudoin under his Iconograph Press imprint. Just before its publication Beaudoin wrote in *Crescendo*:

> We are getting excited about Judson C. Crews.... The rugged quality of his verse, the brittle, metallic brilliance of his language is beginning to have a very specific meaning for us; a something which is making him a strong, significant voice in this year, in this hour, and a voice somehow a little fresher than those we have been accustomed to hearing wailing in the stresses of Pillin, Clayton Stafford, Yvor Winters, and Lincoln Fitzell.[2]

Later in the year, in the book's afterword, Beaudoin added:

> In the ten poems infra you will find as much of Judson C. Crews, honestly disclosed, as I have seen in print. And the Judson C. Crews disclosed, I believe is a rather significant Judson C. Crews. He represents a certain frontier honesty and at the same time a personal development which is peculiar to our immediate year. He is not Vachel Lindsay or Carl Sandburg. He is perhaps something like what they might be were they young men, young poets, now. I like his almost naive vigor whipping his almost suave, urbane

language. I like his natural rhythms and his very cultivated
modulations, his calculated effects.

Greer

Scott Greer reviewed *Psalms for a Late Season* in 1942:

> This is not comforting poetry; it is terrible poetry. It is the
> reflection of the bloody injustice, the legal and illegal murder we
> have known in America, upon an idealist who happens also to be
> a tremendously powerful poet.
>
> Although beautiful, these poems have no embroidery. The
> imagery is a fusion of esthetic beauty and emotional stabbing that
> cuts like a whip. The lines are acid, eating copper, and the music
> is a sparse and certain adaptation of speech rhythms which has no
> hint of softness.
>
> It is regrettable that the pamphlet does not permit a broader
> selection of Crews' work, but from these ten poems a fair estim-
> ate of the fundamental strength of the man is possible. He is a
> poet who realizes what a poet must say and think today. And he
> is a poet who will have much more to say in the future.[3]

Twenty-five years later Greer wrote:

> His poetry, sophisticated and gnostic with a brilliant imagis-
> tic surface, seems to me among the major recent contribu-
> tions to American poetry. He is probably the most widely
> published poet in the country today.[4]

Forbis

In 1952 John Forbis, circulation manager for *Experiment*, a quarterly
of New Poetry, tried to deal with Crews' collection *Come Curse to the
Moon* at some length.

> The work of Judson Crews is a promising sample of Amer-
> ica's fresher poetic talent. He has certain unique abilities
> that are indispensable to the modern, experimental poet—a

shrewd originality of vision and a sure, deft touch with a line. In *Come Curse to the Moon*, his latest, self-edited volume, he uses these gifts so seldom that the appearance of a keen image or a well-wrought line seems almost accidental. The result is a dull and uneven collection of poems.

Crews, as his better poems prove, is quite at home when he deals with the simple. His long suit as a poet is a knack for making the commonplace uncommon, for portraying the usual with an urgency that is arresting and often a bit terrifying. When he assumes sophistication, he goes out on a limb. When he attacks themes profound, prophetic or world-stirring, the limb breaks. *Come Curse to the Moon* is such a broken limb; it has no roots in the simple, brutal, loving earth where Crews belongs. The book is heavy with abstractions and nebulosities which, while they represent a consistent thought, do not represent it poetically.

The selection of the poems included, more than lack of quality is the major weakness of this volume. The poet seems to be trying too hard to press home his point which is essentially a comparison between the "weather of God" and "the weather of eye." What Crews intends is a statement of social ineptitude and man's perceptual limitations seen against the forms of nature and the enigma of the universe. What he achieves is an arrangement of words conveying general cynicism and an inclination toward the ascetic.

The occasional sharp simplicities that characterize poet Crews are lost in the avalanche of unattractive lines and impotent images put there by prophet Crews who is a very self-conscious prophet indeed. The total impression left after a reading of *Come Curse to the Moon* is that the author is like a defiant man hurling BB shot into a cyclone—his armament simply does not measure up to his enemy.[5]

Coffield

The next assessment of any significance was the most extended critique of the range of Crews' poetry that has ever been published. It appeared in 1954, in Glen Coffield's *Criteria For Poetry*. Coffield, poet and editor of the remarkable little mimeograph magazine *The Bridge* and also of *The Grundtvig Review*, was an unusual literary personality and force on the scene of the avant-garde poetry movement after World War II and into the fifties. The list of poets published in his magazines is long, and many of them are well known today: Judson Crews, Mason Jordan Mason, Kenneth Lawrence Beaudoin, Carol Ely Harper, Marion Schoeberlein, Jean Wagner, Larry Eigner, David Cornel De-jong, Kenneth Patchen, Bernard Raymund, William Stafford, Curtis Zahn, Lori Petri, Hyacinthe Hill, K.P.A. Taylor, Stuart Perkoff, Lillith Lorraine, Emily Glen, Cid Corman, Felix N. Stefanile, Lawrence Clark Powell, Ridgely Cummings, Scott Greer, Vincent Ferrini and many others.

Coffield's review was surprising, since he had featured Crews' poetry in many issues of both *The Bridge* and *The Grundtvig Review*. It was an attack on the poet and his poetry. Years later Crews said of it:

> There is certainly some truth in some of it, and I think a good part of my writing in the last twelve years would indicate my own awareness of the truth of some of what he said.[6]

Coffield selected twelve poets to represent the twelve conditioning elements of poetry that he believed needed to be considered in critical evaluation:

1 *Contemporaneity:* Gil Orlovitz
2 *Commonality:* Vincent Ferrini
3 *Belief:* Madeline Gleason
4 *Tradition:* Robert Duncan
5 *Idea:* Kenneth Patchen
6 *Nature:* Wendell Anderson
7 *Language:* Muriel Rukeyser
8 *Technique:* John Walker

By history I mean the chronological record of man and his institutions, and its readiness as example to the poet who has framed pictures of life in his own day and needs to light them more brilliantly by the arc lights of past events. Without historical example the present is likely to seem unimportant, or unrealizable, and such example is then more necessary for contrast when new history is being made....

Although Crews has not made a full or resolved use of historical method, yet in places he has suggested what his or another's poetry might become, if more orderly, and better resolved, and supported by historical example. There are inklings of ideas in his poetry, but he is drunk on the dregs of the symbolists, who have had their day, and so his traceries of meaning remain in the slothful disorder of the unconscious. His profundity, such as it is, is that of random selection, kaleidoscopic accidents, of which one might make endless variations with all kinds of mechanical substitutes for thinking (electronics for example). But an occasional good line is the most that could be hoped for, never a good poem.

Some of his "poetic" interpretations of history:

> The pillaged rebellions are rendered
> the vassals of the towering vessel of wrath

Though the idea may be true, the expression is banal!

> The assassin is terror
> his rich chariots rumbling
> lifting the torture to ultimate law

Better, but too much mouthing of the syllables, too
stultifying in the diction.

> The king and queen ate at table
> with cumquats, hot rolls and berry cider
> and the dwarf (fool to the court) came on crutches
>   they talked
> jovially then of the conquest of Bessarabia

These lines are the best in the book (compare with the first
quoted) and the most sustained passages, probably because
the most natural and straight-forward description. I have no
doubt that Crews could write much more of this kind of
poetry, were he not so unoriginally attached to the affected
and perverse blank page school of art, which based its aesthetics on the sewers of Paris. He is quick to perceive evils,
but his notions of the reasons for them are platitudinous
and limited, over-worked formulas, with which he has felt
so safe, that he has been cautious about extending his
insight.

Crews is of that generation of poets who too often have
held that as long as they could think up neat rationalizations for their detached experiments, that they were
somehow justified. This is not true because too limited. It
is a trick of the lazy, affected, and indifferent. Such rationalizations are merely alibis for (1) neglect of craft, and (2)
mere dabbling in subject matter. And so it becomes apparent that Crews, in his present frame of mind, and attitude,
is not an artist but a dilettante, "one who follows an art or
a branch of knowledge desultorily, or for amusement
only".... He is perhaps the victim of his own philosophy,
which has never shown signs of being really his, but is
merely borrowed, and so does not aptly apply in any sense.
He creates unit by unit instead of unit with unit, and his
sense of creation does not sufficiently extend to what he is
doing with his total production. In other words, he lacks
artistic vision.[7]

Later he comes back to Crews:

The contemporaneity of Crews is like the dregs of the morning coffee. In his poetry are flashbacks to considerations of the early part of the century: surrealism, dadaism, automatic writing, symbolism, imagism, impressionism, existentialism, nihilism, etc.; but he doesn't combine these into a compound, he mixes them in a mixture. He takes summaries of the resolutions of other artists and tries to apply the end results, which is an impossibility; the result of being "widely read in modern," but with little indication of comprising his own elements—except dull repetitions concerning "cold" and the seasons; there would seem to be something pragmatically wrong here, if the results are any indication. His commonality occasionally derives good substance from his observations of the South, and his best opportunity to make a real contribution has always been in this direction, and in descriptions of his boyhood experience, which apparently launched him as a terror. (In one sense, the principle [sic] qualification of a writer is an interesting childhood.) His only belief or faith seems to be in the imitation of other people's ideas; he clings to this as if it were important, whereas it is only worth discarding; most recently, of course, it's existentialism, which was not born in Taos, though an original belief or philosophy could be born in Taos, as anywhere. To do so, however, it would have to grow on the record, as the ideas of Aristotle. (Incidentally, there is a theory that Taos—which was originally Tao, the Spanish added the "s"—got its name from the Chinese religious philosopher, having been brought here centuries ago by the forebears of the Indians.) Crews has little respect for tradition, and as one result of this suffers the usual penalty: of artistic failure. The illusion of independence may seem pleasant at times, but a single individual cannot construct by his own efforts in one lifetime what it took the entire race several centuries to put together. His ideas are mostly superficial observations which lack the depth of learning to give them credence. As

such he is mostly just an agitator, but the natural aspect of
society quickly smooths over every possible kind of
agitation and restores it to calmness. Only a new principle
can embody serious change. His use of nature is largely
generalities, not fine perception, or considered description.
His language is atrocious, really atrocious, for he has alas
sadly stumbled onto Wheelwright's advice, "Make of the
dictionary your Apocalypse!" His technique consists of any
jingling little metric with big words substituted for little
ones. Alice in Wonderland might have written most of his
verses by merely translating James Whitcomb Riley into
polysyllable anonyms. And though by this time it is of no
importance, he completely ignores the matter of spelling.
He uses history, but only by random selection, which is
about the only way he makes use of any subject matter. Before moderns can return to anything like sustained success,
they will have to sustain their study, as well as concentration, to produce form. The gigantic waves of trivia which
we now have are simply due to lack of concentration, and
to the pretentious hope, that by throwing up any kind of
camouflage, the artist can escape the necessary effort for
serious accomplishment. The great error in this is the
failure to realize that sooner or later a critic will come
along ("and classify, boy, classify you right out of existence"—Socrates) who can easily penetrate such sham. Crews
perhaps bases most of his poems on perceptions of failings
in society or other poets, and his poems are largely reactions (rather than creations), and as such he is a slave to the
shortcomings of others. He uses other people's experience
considerably, but mostly for sniping, and the attitudes of
his sniping are largely facile and platitudinous. Saints are
one of his favorite targets, but he has never produced an
original or true insight into the weaknesses of Saints. Often
he merely dredges the ruts of Freud a little deeper without
taking cognizance of, say, Kenneth Burke's sound and
enlightening challenge of Freud's observations on sainthood.
And so for much of Crews' method, one can only muster
a "Ho hum" reaction. Or as Erma Hayden used to say:

4 "Poor little decadent child!" But if he must use random selection instead of serious study, I would suggest that a seventh grade geography might help to break the monotony of much of his recent work.[8]

Kenner

In 1955 Hugh Kenner attempted to summarily dismiss Crews' *The Anatomy of Proserpine*:

> Mr. Crews...is more at home with rough sailor-talk:

> you yellah bastud
> **** you, **** you
> **** jew & jew & jew
> ****allee lousey chink
> **** you, **** you

(The asterisks are his). The *Anatomy of Proserpine* confines its attention to specialized zones:

> Your bosom is not home
> your **** could never be

Elsewhere we read how

> She lashed against the mast
> her neurotic bums goosefleshed in the shivery
>   dawn
> Wobber came to her and left her trembling
> and Arnold came and Hatch
> and Doyle shamefaced....

We learn no more of these worthies, unless they are the ones in another poem who "talked of ****." Another persona is more literary, or maybe just drunk:

> December lost so ever thus

curled in love though Shirl left thus
thane we leapt the river thus
thane we slept in every lust

Thong for thane
the thigh be girth
girt we are against bold lust

Periodically there turns up a figure with the entrancing
name of Bulltoven, of whom one would like to hear
more.... If the bourgeois aren't épatéd by [him] it's no use.

Kenner concludes his article by conceding, after this shock to his staid,
academic sensibilities, that "Mr. Crews can be an impressively lively
writer between asterisks."[9]

Whetstone

Also in 1955 Jack Lindeman and Edgar H. Schuster, the editors of
Whetstone, reviewed *The Anatomy of Proserpine* in an omnibus review
entitled "A Variety of Poets":

One comes away from Mr. Crews' poems as one would
leave the deck of a ship for solid land following a prolonged
sea voyage. And though the poems, themselves, are set
against a not uncharacteristic (for the times) background of
Freudian psychology, the mood being established by a brief
introductory quotation from the master, himself, the sexual
symbolism, despite its obviousness, is almost never allowed
to blunt the poignant effects of the sea. That Mr. Crews
intended it thus we have no reason to doubt, for he
explains in "Elpinore's Overland Putsch" that

This is not a theme of love but of the sea
chaos a part of my design.

The chaos of love and of the sea are fused excitingly in a
constant imagery of lust and longing, interrupted, though
not distorted, by occasional ironies such as:

It was deathly silent
                    except for the rats
gnawing the tarped cargo of coffins
the returned heroes from Okinawa....

The sea is female to all men's desires...

but she was sick and without
a private chamber
            her menses
betraying her at last
            our lusts
but whetted by her fear.

Granted that Mr. Crews' concept is not original, his language and manner strikes [sic] one quite squarely with the
sheer force of individuality. As poet, he is neither an
imitator nor is he easily imitated.[10]

Eckman

In 1958 Frederick Eckman wrote a critique of one of Crews' poems,
"Cold for Night and Lasting."

Finally we come to automatic writing (or so I interpret the
source of this poem), where little more than the illusion of
coherence is maintained. The series of images hold together,
if at all, by a design that is totally graphic. From this point
surrealism, unable to go further in language, disappears
totally into painting.

Cold for Night and Lasting

The striped want permeates the dawn

the throne is stippled with waiting

The cart of the beggar is waiting
branded with the severed eye

Rain is waiting but the moon is low
its severed side is touched by wind

Here, restless mind, is your hunger
the hangman loving your restless side

The hangers are broken and gutted
the wretched have lost all but their will

Mail is smeltered by waiting, willing
wanting is marked by the severed eye

lasting is marked by the severed year

The substantive method, as we have seen, produces an
array of poems so diverse that generalization becomes nearly impossible. Certain broad patterns, however, can be dis-
cerned. First, let us consider its weaknesses, which I have
not demonstrated at length in the text only because they
have been so frequently pointed out in the past, by every
genteel critic from Henry James onward.

At its unimaginative worst, the substantive poem can be
quite as drab and monotonous as poor decorative verse is
brittle and affected. By clinging too close to his presenta-
tional method, the poet produces mere dull reportage or
unimaginative amateur photography. At another extreme,
the outer reaches of surrealism sometimes betray an irre-
sponsibility to language and image that is either infuriating
or comic, depending on the reader's immediate frame of
mind. Of the three modes, concretive verse makes fewest
prosodic demands (there are, naturally, brilliant exceptions),
and such indifference can lead either to the dull thumpty-
thud of tin-ear iambics or, worse, to a species of chopped

chopped up, rhythmless lines that are neither good prose nor good verse. I should imagine that this mode harbors more out-and-out incompetents than any other, if that means anything.

Its strengths, on the other hand, are considerable. At best it has a bold catholicity, which scorns nothing that might serve as material for a poem and can often wrest poetry from the most uncompromising subjects. It has a rich immediacy of presentation, the result of its loyalty to the poetic image. And it possesses a flexibility of *genre* which allows it to range with the greatest freedom between fact and fantasy, dream and drama, sanity and madness. As I have said earlier, it is the great common style of American poetry in the first half of the century—the matrix from which all other contemporary styles, however indirectly, proceed.[11]

May

James Boyer May, poet and editor of *Trace*, reviewed *The Feel of Sun and Air upon her Body* in 1960:

Whatever may be said of Crews, in terms of analysis, his every word poetically *happens*. Crews stands confirmed a Poet, regardless. This selection shows that he has become more self-critical and is doing more self-editing.[12]

De Witt

A refutation of Coffield's strictures can be found in the remarkable explication by G. De Witt of Crews' poem, "Deception of Eve," which appeared in *Blue Guitar* in 1961. This explication, the only textual analysis in depth of Crews' poetry that has been published until now, reveals an advanced overall point of view not only on the meaning of poetry, but on the meaning of life as well. De Witt approached the poem at its face value.

First the poem itself.

Deception of Eve

Deceptive the passion lane
apples where her breasts
basketed dulce oblong
held in where she stood

Flavored the arbor loom
dulce in spark and heft
wreath the night is fold
firm in the ground of pain

Girded or held in growth
does fever yet remind
sold ever out and outward
thus dulce part through myth

For whom the leaf engaged
Smother whom in love be held
apple of the breast and young
bask in dulce crowned.

De Witt's explication:

The phrasal structures in "Deception of Eve" release the
full image. The poem contains very few conceptual impurities and therefore comes very close to presenting itself as a
single, fused image. The substantives, unimpaired by
predicates, are full and multivalent in their import and
impact. The progressions are not broken or inflated by conceptual lines and abstract diction. The success of this
organic poem rests at least in part upon its syntax.

The plot of the poem is simple: it tells the story of the
Fall and its consequences. However, the poem begins, in
effect, in the fifth act—as Gray said of the ballad. The deed
has been done (for to trace the events would be to narrate,
and narration, using the clause in time sequence, works
against the poem as space object). The complications arising

from the deed are taken up immediately after the nature of the act has been established. In the first stanza Eve has in effect exchanged her breasts for apples. The second stanza makes clear the meaning of the exchange: Eden is the "ground" or area where "pain" began for mankind. The apples, although natural on the tree, are unnatural on Eve, who through the exchange has lost her primitive attributes and attitudes. Since the apples come from the Tree of Knowledge, Eve has exchanged her perceptual self for a conceptual symbol. The movement from percept to concept, initiated in Eden, is the beginning of "pain." The third stanza points out that for mankind the status of Eve before the pain began is now but a vague memory and that sweetness ("dulce") is gone with the myth of Adam and Eve. In the final stanza we are reminded of just how much has been lost. The leaf suppresses and stifles natural, sweet love, for sweetness and innocence are now confined to the young. In a word, the plot concerns itself with the aftermath of the Fall, not with the actions involved in the Eden story itself. Thus, the poet avoided the need for narrative—and along with it the need for the clause.

Since "Deception" is primarily phrasal, we are able to descend from the plot and work directly with the full import of each substantive. For example, "passion lane" has at least three referents: Literally, it is the path Eve took in the Garden of Eden. But it is also the journey of Christ (the stations of the cross constitute a "passion lane"). Further, it refers to the path down which man has gone as a result of accepting the Judeo-Christian mythic. In all three cases at least two meanings of "passion" (emotion, sexual desire, and suffering) apply. The term "deceptive" indicates that all three "lanes"—Eve's, Christ's, and man's—have been in some way misleading, have ensnared us all. Apples, gained at the price of losing the innocent sweetness of the apple-like breasts (which serve as a synecdoche for the inviting, unsullied, fresh fullness of natural woman and therefore natural desire) are no substitutes for the "dulce oblongs" which were from the beginning an organic part of woman.

Her breasts, "held in"—from within—by her own somatic structure, are a natural part of her. The apples, however, are separate and had to be taken mechanically and held externally—the original "falsies."

Ripping the apples from *their* own organic growth was an unnatural act and "Flavored the arbor loom"—befouled (one meaning of "flavor") the garden while at the same time giving forth a pleasant aroma—as some plants do when mutilated or plucked. The lush weight ("heft") and shine ("spark") of the apple are soon obscured by the writhing ("wreath")—the movement of the serpent—night, the darkness of evil and sin. The basis ("ground") for the continuing penalty ("pain") of all mankind has now been established.

Now Eve, like all mankind, is clothed ("girded") and restrained ("held in"), for she has, by accepting the Old-Testament meaning of her act, sacrificed ("sold") to God ("ever out and outward") the natural sweetness of innocent passion and sensuality. By accepting the "myth" (the Bible story of the Fall and the Redemption) man has parted with or sold his natural pleasure and primitive human situation ("thus dulce part through myth"). "Part" also means "break" or "put asunder," which is to say that man as an organic creature has now split himself away from a vital part of his own nature.

The last stanza reveals the final consequences of this split. The leaf symbolizes the artificial attitude of Adam and Eve after the Fall. It has bound ("engaged") them to an artificial condition which stifles or suppresses ("smother") natural and full impulses of love and desire. "Leaf" also denotes "page," referring to the written myth, the Bible, which has restrained those who accept the Judeo-Christian interpretation of human existence. Those who behold ("be held") the apple-like breasts, i.e., are excited by desire, are unnaturally restrained. The young, however, enjoy the natural warmth of desire ("young/bask in dulce crowned") before their natural instincts are smothered by their reading of the myth. However, this line may be taken another way:

we are all the "young"—the offspring—of Adam and Eve;
therefore we are smitten ("bask"—"bash") by the sexless
sweetness of the Redemption. ("Crowned" also means
"bashed"). The crown of thorns is not the same as a
"wreath" (second stanza) of living garlands in Eden. Thus
the natural sweetness of the original state has been
"crowned"—cut at the root (a crown—graft)—and a substitute for sensual, human nature grafted onto it. But the
roots of emotion are still there ("does fever yet remind"),
and the noun "smother" denotes a smoldering fire.

The poem, then, concerns the Redemption as deception.
But to state the theme as a proposition and to force the perceptual terms into clauses would be to shear off and flatten
the rich multivalencies of the poem. Not only would the
multivalent properties suffer, but also the numerous
progressions of image. The central progression is that of
pleached vegetation. The first stanza presents "basketed,"
the noun of which denotes a container woven of straw. The
basket is for apples, inorganically ripped from the tree and
deposited in a container woven of *dead* and *dried* vegetation.
This dead weaving contrasts dramatically with the pleached
green of the "arbor loom," the intertwined and living bower
of Eden. The woven straw also contrasts with "wreath";
however, this term also denotes a laurel of mourning (and
therefore death), indicating the "death" of natural man in
the paradoxical context of Eden's green life. "Fold" means
"intertwine"; "wreath the night is fold" thus suggests that
an artificial pleaching has occurred: the "wreath" or
"writhe" of the serpent embracing or intertwining with Eve.
"Fold" also means "enclose," as with wickerwork—again,
dead material. "Girded" means "enclosed"—holding in or
covering Eve's natural "growth"—the naturally tangled
pubic hair becomes a "held-in growth." One meaning of
"engaged" in the final stanza is "entangled" or "meshed,"
but here in the sense of an unnatural binding or restraint.
Finally in the last line of the poem the pleached-vegetation
progression is resolved: "bask in dulce crowned." The
natural human emotions and sensual sweetness ("dulce") are

cut at the roots, and another plant is crown-grafted onto the stem: the crown of thorns worn by Christ as he traversed the "deceptive...passion lane." This crown, like the basket that held the apples—the breast-substitutes—is woven of dead, dried materials. Unlike the basket straw, however, the thorns hurt.

Through this long progression of pleached materials, the poet has established his main metaphor, which organizes the whole poem: naturally entwined, living vegetation—as in the "arbor loom" of Eden—is likened to the natural, sensually organic human condition; conversely, the dead and dry woven artifacts—baskets and crowns—are like the dead and dry or bloodless "loom" of the Judeo-Christian myth of man, his Fall and Redemption. This two-part metaphor presents perceptual relationships which fuse into a single image, a verbal ikon founded on the phrase. This ikon presents what Swinburne proposed:

> Thou has conquered, O pale Galilean;
> The world has grown gray from thy breath.[13]

Michaelson

Also in 1961 L.W. Michaelson, then at Colorado University, had this to say about Crews' *Inwade to Briney Garth*:

> But this Judson is of the blood, flesh, bone, womb and let-us-not-have-any-clichés-in-my-verse school, sired maybe by Dylan Thomas, with a dash of the beatnicks, or pre-beatniks à la Max Bodenheim....
>
> He likes warm, fleshy-bloody words, and he uses them well, in fact, there's something of the old Renaissance love of words here. I mean, Crews does like the sound, the taste and feel of words; he drives them before his pen with whip and they bounce, squirm and joggle; in short, they're kooky in the good sense of the word.[14]

Creeley

The poet Robert Creeley has written of Crews' work several times in the last three decades. First in 1961:

> Judson Crews has, for some time now, lived outside of the common areas of recognition, surviving by his persistence and by, as well, the respect those who have read his work with care have come to give. He asks for nothing and lives sparely in his work, a place for survival, where the test of a life is that which is possible in it, terrors of image, dream sensualities, hard thought, all given place. The twists of language ...define this same character of test, of meaning, curiously, of statement against statement, word against word.[15]

The latest, in 1978:

> Mr. Crews is not so simply an autobiographical writer, and I don't know whether or not he's done all the things he talks of in these poems. I'm damn sure someone has—and that their wry, laconic, sensitive perception is fact of very human experience. *Integrity* is a very apt word for Judson Crews' way of being human. He won't do what he doesn't believe in doing, nor will he say something for simple convenience. That's cost him a lot of times, jobs included, but you can no more be a little bit committed to telling the veritable truth than you can be a little bit pregnant. So you might as well go for broke....
>
> I'm sure that Judson Crews will be both remembered and honored for the loner wisdom of what he had to tell us and that wild down-home elegance of what one might call his delivery.... Maybe it will take time to catch up with this dear man's delights. But if you're reading this, you're surelygetting close. Onward![16]

Scott

Winfield Townley Scott reviewed *Hermes Past the Hour* in 1963.

Judson Crews' work--in its various aspects--continues to charm me. And by that I mean not only what he writes in his poems but how he presents them. Every few years Crews gathers up a bunch of poems which have mostly been published in little magazines—he is in the Great Tradition of the Little Magazine—and makes them into a book from his own press in Taos. And here is a brand new book.

It is, as customary with Crews, spiral-bound in illustrated cardboard. It is spiced with several full-page photographs in the nude. The poems are set in various kinds of type, and they run to zany titles; for instance: Weep the Mulberry Ladder, World From the Pelvic Arch, Rachel the Wicked Pie, Rattle Roon Hoady, and The Bale of Brine the Quaver Reaching.

All these facets of presentation are in a sense emanations of the poetry, which of course is the important thing. The poems tend to be sensual and sensuous, vigorous, quick; and whether their tone is loving or loathing they may be said to be on the side of life.

Crews has an ear:

> Smear like the stone of crucifixion
> rain has limbered the wonder
> hinder is soft as the cormorants
> drifting on the lavender screaming.

Or, again:

> Hear the surf boom
> and watch kelp mingle
> twine and retwine
> pattern its rank maze.

And sometimes the powerful statement:

> his blood
> ate the snow away for a little while and then was stone
> itself as the night came.[17]

Blazek

In 1967 Douglas Blazek reviewed *You, Mark Antony, Navigator Upon the Nile* and *Angels Fall, They are Towers*:

I think the reason Judson Crews has never shot any of us off our bar stools or office chairs is because we don't exactly know what he is doing. We don't quite understand; yet we do know he is writing poetry and that some of it carves a clean incision 3 inches between the ribs. He is a mystery without being a mystery. He has his own personal thing going that makes no real loud noises, nor any real quiet squeaks. He works alone and this, to most of us, is synonymous with outdatedness...to be a Mover of Minds one must be in social and critical circles, one cannot respect a soft vague blur from New Mexico. HUMBUG! as Scrooge would proclaim; a poet working with himself may not make a big splash but he will find something of much greater significance; what he must say, how it must be said.

Crews writes about 25% in marvelous performance, about 50% in mediocre performance and about 25% in disingenuous hack performance. The last 75 percent can be seen in all his books, these withstanding, and I get to wondering if he isn't writing a poem just to write a poem, the way a housewife will dust a vase she dusted before in order to save her from the trap of silence and emptiness.

It's the first magical/marvelous 25% that makes all of his books worth reading and buying (some books are worth reading but not buying). If he doesn't get you with a hot piece of lead ("My New Revelation for the Day") he'll get you with language snorting through your mind like a thousand lawn mowers ("The River of Mirth").

The only substantial difference in these two books is
that *Angels* has better nudes than *Mark Antony*.[18]

Smith, Whitebird, Bergé

D. Vincent Smith, poet and editor of *The Human Voice Quarterly,
Olivant Quarterly* and other magazines, wrote in 1968 that Crews was
"a major American poetic figure.... Quick and swash-buckling with
language, an experimenter in the true sense."[19]

In her 1979 introduction to *Greasybear Songs*, Joanie Whitebird commented on Crews' method in transcribing poetry of a Navajo Indian
client when he was a community coordinator for the New Mexico
State Hospital and a lecturer at the branch college of the University of
New Mexico in Gallup.

> He is an established poet with a complete symbology of his
> own. But it is only his years of work on paper that give us
> the trust in his knowledge of the translation of these sym-
> bols. In this collection of poems, Charley John Greasybear
> creates in a language of awareness both different and more
> extensively interwoven than our own. And Judson records
> and renders it with precision.[20]

Carol Bergé wrote the introduction to Crews' 1983 collection of
poems, *The Clock of Moss*, giving voice to her perception of him as a
poet:

> Judson Crews, master of the sensual poem, fascinates the
> reader in his ability to extend tactile values to earth itself:
> the landscape's features to be studied and delighted in, as
> much for the challenges as for the satisfactions. With this
> book, Crews steps into a rare and discrete pantheon of
> American poets who have the ability to move out of the
> mechanized assumptions and back to weather and land as
> causes of the deeper human responses....
>   The poems acknowledge Judson Crews' scholarly
> capabilities in sociology. His Everyman is Woman as well,
> moving from a central feeling or event as set into desert or

mountain landscape, and found later as sepia tintype, Daguerrotype or photogrammetry. As a man more absorbed in integrity than attracted to superfice or the occasion, his motive is to become part of the subject in its own time. The pleasure of discovery is accessed through the travails of his characters. We are enabled to enter the adventure.[21]

The Last Decade

His reputation is building. In his first 43 years of publication only eight collections of his poems issued from presses other than his own. In the last fourteen years there have been eleven, including the 122-page *The Noose: a Retrospective—4 Decades, The Clock of Moss* from Boise State University, reprint editions of two of his earlier books, and two magazine issues devoted exclusively to his poetry. In 1986 he attracted an overflow audience to hear him read in the annual Writers' Week at the University of California, Riverside, and to cheer at the mention of Bulltoven.

In 1991 there appeared three significant comments. First, the poet R.P. Dickey wrote an extended review of *A Unicorn When Needs Be*:

> Every poem in the book is a work of art. Of course, that is something one could say, and ought to say, about any book of poems....
>
> If a book of poems has only one poem in it that is good, i.e., rereadable, then that book justifies its physical existence. This book by Crews has more than one.
>
> He loves English, and sometimes in a poem he lolls the language around with his tongue in a high, self-pleasuring, comic-mandarin style not unlike that of Wallace Stevens....
>
> There is a lot of variety in this collection of vintage Judson Crews. Let me take up the rest of the space in this brief notice with "If I Have Not Praised." It is Crews at the top of his bent. Read it aloud slowly, at the top of your bent and enjoy a classically pure lyric poem of the highest order:

> If I take
> some twigs of elder

and build an altar

All your own
oh the sun
will rise and set

Exactly there
and stars
will settle there

The cool moon
will wash upon
this altar

And small fawns
suckle
its sweet fronds

You only
will spurn its site
sightless forever[22]

Later the same year a staffer on *The Plastic Tower* had this to say
about *Blood Devisible By Sand*:

Read this chapbook and despair, oh ye poets of free
verse. Some poems in *Blood Devisible By Sand* will make
just about anyone look foolish by comparison. Crews is a
rock of alternative poetry; he's been doing good stuff for
fifty years. Of course, over that span of time, he's laid his
share of eggs, and tossed off some awkward chapbooks.
This ain't one of them.

Crews is mean and spare with his words, and the poetry
in here is boiled down to an essence. Some of these poems
say more in 10 words than other poets say in 10 pages. And
yet he still manages to be lyrical, as in "It Is Good, Pulling
the Curtains Back While": "The light is still congealed like

pale smoke/among the naked branches of a few/Dark trees. It's past the solstice and the sun."

The chapbook contains Crews' usual assortment of naked-women-and-sex poems, but there's lots more, including a rare nostalgia piece called "So, Rexroth," and he skewers a couple well-known poets in "I've Never Won a Prize and Wouldn't." *Blood Devisible by Sand* is on the money, an example of A-1 poetry.[23]

In another 1991 issue of the same magazine, a review of *A Unicorn When Needs Be* summarized the poet's career.

For the latter part of this century, Judson Crews has been one of the finest "unknown" poets to toil the small press venue. Judging by some of his recent chapbooks, he is more on top of the scene than ever.

A Unicorn When Needs Be is recommended for anyone even passingly familiar with Crews' recent work. This chapbook was originally published in 1963, and the new reprint is a nice insight into Crews' work and style from nearly three decades ago. Not only that, but the poems still stand up today, and many of them are excellent by any standards.

The poems in *Unicorn* are as tough as a two-dollar steak. Compared to Crews' current poems, they seem blunter yet wordier; hard-hitting and sharp, and at the same time more verbose and circuitous. Over the last 30 years, his work has gotten sparer, leaner, as if he was constantly struggling to say more in fewer words.

Some of this could be due to the era in which *Unicorn* was written; the more verbose poems have beat and abstract influences to them. But these poems are definitely *not* Ginsberg rip-offs. Some are, to be sure, a bit self-possessed, but there's much less of the grandstanding and moon-baying in these than in the beat poems of the era.

A number of these poems are still standouts, including "Port Wound Bracing Loss" in particular, "An Insistence

On Climate" and "Of Credible Beatitudes." All in all a chapbook that has held its own over the test of time.[24]

The following year the appearance of *Henry Miller and my Big Sur Days: Vignettes from Memory* provided the opportunity for a number of reviewers to belatedly acknowledge the importance of Crews' poetry. Shelby Stephenson called him "a creator of lyrics hardened and polished in a speech which is music, metaphysical and muscular at the base." Catherine Lynn wrote that "he possesses authentic and lasting greatness," and Ron Androla: "I believe there is nobody quite like Judson Crews on the face of our planet, a major American poet...a surviving prophet."[25]

His stature continues to grow. In the Summer 1993 issue of *Atom Mind*, editor Gregory Smith wrote:

> I recall when I cranked up *Atom Mind* for the first go-'round in the late 1960s receiving submissions of poems from Crews.... I was thrilled that he had chosen to honor my struggling little magazine with his work, because then, as well as for decades prior and decades after, Judson Crews has been foremost among this nation's "little-mag" poets....
>
> I am proud to have Judson Crews as the featured poet in this issue's The Living Poets Series. Read his poetry, which spans more than six decades of insightful writing...and be certain, as I am, that somewhere in the annals of Twentieth Century American Literature there is a prominent place reserved for Judson Crews.[26]

Finally, from Mark Weber's introduction to the latest collection of Crews' poetry, *Mannequin Anymore That*:

> An experimenter goes forward, his dick like a hungry arrow with a face on it. His poems know more than he does....
>   ...Ole Judson is a scientist. His poems done swiggled around in a test tube and poured out on a petrie dish, aromae of cunt and algae, lichen & moss, rocks, juices...a gathering of queries where he uses no question marks....

We see here enclosed a later version of his fictitious character Bulltoven.... At the earliest [January 1948] he says [Bulltoven] was attributed to a mixture of Creeley and Olson, "Creeley, though younger than me, a sort of father figure." Other times he says Bulltoven [was] a type of veteran colonel of the Boer Wars. And finally, "The trouble with Bulltoven is in my later poems he became like myself"....

Generally speaking one could say Judson is a modernist. How modern can poetry get? the oldest of literate forms. Judson's themes go farther back. Borrowing nothing from the wasted and forlorn his work never fails to go forth. He's always right there to smell the daisies. And loving every minute of it.[27]

Tributes

In addition to reviews and articles on Judson Crews—the man, the poet, the artist—poems testifying to his influence as a writer have been dedicated to him by Scott Greer, Robert Burlingame and D. Vincent Smith. (In addition, Beaudoin prefaced his poem "From letters for 7 exiled: iii." with the words: "for J.C. on the plains.") I include these here, along with two general articles which may serve to give us a certain summary of the man's place as a poet and artist in our time, and to highlight some of the critical material in the preceding chapter.

Greer

Scott Greer has dedicated three poems to Crews: "Pearl Harbor Day, Dec. 7, 1941," "To Judson in Taos" (which spawned a response from John Atkins, "To Judson in Chaos," in a later issue of Crews' own magazine, *Suck-Egg Mule*), and the following:

Augury
For J.C.C.

They screamed murder at the strength of their lungs,
But some were still as stone;
The sheep quivered terror and huddled together,
But some were ever alone.

Like a pale strong vine, caught in a ledge,
Alive between earth and stone,
While a sea tore around them, dark and wild,
Some were quiet, and pliant, and alone.

And tides of time washed with the sun,
And cities flowered to ruin;
The moment come in the future and gone—
The murder again, and soon, and soon.

Tell you the future will rise with the dawn,
Tell you to die for the proof?
I will tell you that some have the strength of stone,
And truth is not killed in the root.[28]

Burlingame

Robert Burlingame visited Taos in June 1966, and while there wrote
this tribute.

Sober Poem
(for Judson Crews)

I read his book my friend's
and wish only to tell him that it is good
very good but not his

anymore than the leaves
on the most discrete tree belong to it
they belong to me
to the shade they create

to all the children who do not thank it
even as they play beneath it
or use its great limbs

it looks at me as I read it
and lets me use it as a shade against
the sun.[29]

Smith

D. Vincent Smith wrote a poem which, he said, "was plain and simply about Judson and his influence on American writing."[19]

It is Mostly a Matter of Praise Life
--for anybody but: Judson Crews

Crews is an important man. What I
Remember most about him was his hair--
Black and straight. And the poems
(so *unlike* him, Bob Nystedt said
in his apartment in N.Y. or was it
in my apartment in Atlanta, Bob,
with you and Elaine...all 3 of us &
Olivant broke?—I gained weight for the first
time in my life...and Maud kind
enough to us to say to you and
Elaine "come live with me" and be
my pedigree but don't burn the free midnight
oil for sleeping the sun away)!!!
In *Three Hands*: always writing about the sea
& he so far away. How may one speak
(these days) without involving others
so deeply a part of one's own life? But
Now may one speak of the "failures" one is
so fond of speaking of, those things reputedly
One learns by? And I had thought one learned
Only by one's successes. Anyhow,
I was about to tell you something about Crews

(J.C., in the '40's, when he was appearing
Like a live duck or a mad guinea in *The
Westminster*), Oh well, not over a page
Long. I suppose I've said it anyhow.[30]

MacNab

Arden MacNab interviewed Crews at his Taos home in 1965. The
result was the following article:

Henry Miller says of Taos poet Judson Crews, in his
book *Big Sur and the Oranges of Hieronymus Bosch*,
"Judson Crews of Waco, Texas, one of the first to muscle
in, reminded one—because of his shaggy beard and
manner of speech—of a latter day prophet. He lived
almost exclusively on peanut butter and wild mustard
greens and neither smoked nor drank."

Only the beard has disappeared—the intense poet
remains.

At his adobe in Taos, where he has lived eighteen
years, one is immediately impressed by his ragged
vitality. Standing over six feet, dressed in blue jeans and
wearing a greying crew-cut, he twangs with laconic East
Texas drawl details about his life.

When I was an undergraduate at Baylor
University I did a lot of preaching, but I
regard this period as having interfered with
my development as a poet.

...Throughout the last twenty-five years Crews has
published his poems rather consistently in over two-
hundred little magazines. His books of poetry number
twelve. However, it is doubtful if you will find any of
Crews' books at the book stores. One reason for this
could be his use of nude photographs with his poetry,
which always prompts the question: "Why?"

In response, Crews says,

> I use pictures. Certain of them are nudes.
> There is no definite reason. They serve to
> deflect the average reader that the book is
> not for, anyway.

Dr. John Biggers, the Head of the Art Department at Texas Southern University in Houston, exclaimed on seeing one of Crews' books containing poetry and nudes, "Why, this man is presenting the garden of life!"

Poet Robert Creeley said in a review of Crews in the magazine *Poetry*, "*The Heart in Naked Hunger* and *The Feel of Sun and Air Upon Her Body* have this hardihood of thought; and both as well use the device of occasional photographs, nudes, of flat building fronts, of many untoward things, let us say, to shock the mind awake by a somewhat wry invitation."

One feels that Crews is doing in his own field what Henry Miller has done in his.

Winfield Townley Scott has said of his poetry that "the logic is a logic of images." And sounds can produce images, as in "Pastoral":

> Father, father, the name of sorrow
> daffodil gathering by the glade
>
> Mother, mother, the wicked sparrow
> the song he made did pierce my heart
>
> Brother, brother, the earth is ended
> night has swept the wretched tomorrow
>
> Sister, sister, swear on my heart
> no daffodil ever shall brighten your braid

Crews can be humorous with a Hamlet humor, as in "Citadel of Breathless Wonder":

> The wind ballooning her loose skirts
> pink against a pink sunset

Turning quickly she called me a — — — — —

What made her think that perhaps she had wanted to eat
    out
and later go to a movie

Now the stage is set
for a quiet evening at home

Or lyrical in a modern way, as in "The Gull is By the Sea":

The gull is by the sea:
in blue stemmings of tide
rising,
to white breakers
lowering.

There are many wings
pinioned—

            many, many wings
dipped to the low wind:
where the wild water's
genesis?

Yonder

are many, many wings
and a white crane

When questioned about his method of producing
poetry Crews replied that it was his habit to work
intensively for two or three days two or three times a
year, with the result that he occasionally produced thirty
or forty poems in a week-end.

As to why he is an artist he quoted Otto Rank's
remark that the artist in society is a neurotic and a
misfit. He added, however, that the largest neurotic body
in the country consists of the common laborer. In other

words, the lower you go on the economic scale, the more you encounter the neurotic.

Do Crews' poems have a message? Not if you consider message in any literal sense or if you feel message has to be concerned with social themes. Crews believes that for all purposes the political-social battles are won—the Civil Rights situation merely represents a cultural lag—and that what should concern one now are interpersonal relationships, evolvement of sensibility and the prevailing bourgeoisness—a condition which implies no further evolvement, since the bourgeoisie have reached their standards. In this context, the "Berkeley Rebels" are of more significance than the Civil Righters, who, in the final analysis, are demanding the right to be bourgeois.

Although Crews has been influenced by William Carlos Williams, Wallace Stevens, Ezra Pound, Kenneth Fearing and others, he writes, as anyone who has worked seriously in any art, in an idiom of his own. He remains current and persistent and promises to be one of the United States' foremost poets in the next few years.[31]

Foster

Joseph O'Kane Foster paid the following tribute on the occasion of the departure of Crews and his family from Taos after almost twenty years.

Last Monday morning one of Taos' most important people slipped quietly out of town.

I refer to Judson Crews....

His circle of poet-friends in America is enormous. While they lived in Taos, Judson and Mildred Crews' house was a sympathetic and meaningful gathering place for artists and writers.

I have always felt finer after talking to Judson Crews. He was a spiritual Gibraltar in our midst. He had great

profundity, and a sense of honor that is virtually unknown in the modern world.

His poetry—? It is called obscure. So was Joyce when
we first read him. And Galileo's ideas must certainly
have been obscure to the poor people of Pisa. Obscurity
is the complaint of those who want only to indulge
themselves in the old ways of feeling in art.

Judson worked on the unknown frontiers of man's
consciousness—where nothing is known and all is
waiting to be discovered.

He had many brilliant successes. He was powerful
and unbelievable in the effects he achieved—graceful
sleight of hand tricks of the soul.

I do not think anyone since Blake[32] has matched more
beautiful rhythms to the spirit's unfolding than Judson
Crews.

For sheer originality in the procreative sense Crews
is unequalled in the world of poetry today. The diffi-
culty, the perplexity of some of his poems is only evid-
ence to me of his evolutionary greatness.

At his best Crews achieves vivid pictures of great
metaphysical serenity. He is a master at merging the sensuous and the colloquial into something transcendental.
He has an intense ethnic understanding of national character in artistic terms.

He is consummately skillful in this new Modernity of
the soul. A technical virtuoso. Today—expertly spiritual-
ized.

Yet for all his genius he is artless, plain spoken. He
fails and fails yet suddenly triumphs. And it is worth
waiting for these fair passages to find their way to your
heart.

He stands, then, primarily for the freeing of the spirit
of man in its widest sense.

Modern poets are still concerned with what is the
proper subject for poetry. Crews' answer is very simple.
This world in terms of the Other world. His translation
from the literal to the sublime is breath-taking. From

confusion, vulgarity, the completely unimportant to a new world, a new imagery which he makes unmistakably manifest and beautiful.

Crews is working on a religion of everyday life. This is no easy task for in the present complex anarchy deeper meanings are hidden from us. Meaning for Crews is something richer, more significant, more magnificent than the intellect. He is submerged and functions from immeasurable depths.

Judson Crews wrestles with his Dream as Jacob did with his angel.

Faulkner's Dream, thoroughly in possession of him, is vastly beyond him. It is sweeping and saturated with beautiful details Faulkner himself can hardly be credited with. The "South." The South. Hemingway (always reader-aware) constructed his Dream self-consciously. Hemingway's Dream is confused and finite—purposely commonplace. Each polished sentence Hemingway adds only limits his Dream. Hemingway became a victim of his own style. The defects of Hemingway's Dream are the defects of life...Hemingway's own personal defects. Hemingway died because he never had an organic Dream to sustain him. Hemingway had no spiritual continuum.

Judson Crews' Dream is a sort of inchoation before our very eyes. It has being suddenly and prevails over our ordinary conception of life. Some of his effects are prodigious—flagrantly beautiful. And of course, sex is ever the talisman.

Meaning in Crews' poems rises as new islands in the sea. Meanings are not structurally capable of survival and subside again and are lost. But even though they have disappeared they have left us something to wonder about: Judson's tremendous symbol-ridden world.

It is this unexpected, passing nature of Crews' vision (an *awhile*-world) that is so disturbing yet so exciting. His poems are classic fragments of a vast symposium on life he is assembling. We must examine them, decipher them a little like the chunks of marble in the Roman Forum for clues to a grandeur beyond. We become finer, larger deciphering Judson Crews' poems as his meaning gradually enlarges itself—becomes a valid presence in our minds. Of the few writers who have made their home in Taos I consider Crews second only to D.H. Lawrence in literary achievement.

Surely it is time now for a carefully selected volume of Crews' poems to appear.

Although Judson Crews is for the moment doomed to obscurity because of the peculiar structure of our Commercial-industrial culture, he is, nevertheless, among the neglected elite of our society.

I feel very sad that Taos has lost a man as great as Judson Crews.

Now that Judson has gotten over Taos—its deceptive fascination—he will soon become a national figure, conceivably the poet of our Times.[33]

Notes

1. Judson Crews has assisted the author in all possible ways, in particular making available those of his letters not yet deposited in libraries. Crews' personal papers are scattered among the Humanities Research Center of the University of Texas at Austin, the Special Collections Department of the University of California at Los Angeles, the Beinecke Library at Yale, and the University of New Mexico. The author also acknowledges the assistance of A. Wilber Stevens, who founded *Interim* (1944-1954) and in 1968 edited an anthology entitled *Poems Southwest*; Marvin Malone, editor of the *Wormwood Review*; William E. Taylor of Stetson University; Joel Olimengaga, poet and editor; Joseph Colin Murphy, poet and editor of *Whetstone*; and the poet William Stafford.

2. *Crescendo* 1(4):13, Spring 1942. Like Crews, Beaudoin has had to publish much of his poetry at his own expense, despite its high quality. He responded to the author's inquiry with a memoir of Crews, quoted above in Chapter 1.

3. *Crescendo* 1(5):15-16, Summer 1942. Scott Greer, who was then editing *Crescendo*, is an old friend of Judson Crews, as are Kenneth Beaudoin and A. Wilber Stevens. Dr. Greer, later Chair of the Department of Metropolitan Studies of Northwestern University, is a well-known poet and has appeared for decades in the literary magazines, in addition to publishing a number of books in his field, sociology, particularly metropolitan sociology.

4. Letter to the author, August 3, 1968.

5. *Experiment* 6(2):63, 1952.

6. Letter to the author, August 1, 1968.

7. *Criteria for Poetry*, p. 144-145. Coffield lived in a Thoreauvian fashion in an old house in the forest outside of Portland, Oregon. How he managed to eke out an existence and perform the amount of work he did is a mystery to many. He lived on a shoestring, working at odd jobs in the neighborhood whenever necessary. He picked blueberries in season and existed on a blueberry-pie dough concoction and from the fruits of a small vegetable plot.

8. *Ibid.*, p. 164-165.

9. *Poetry* 86(4):244-247, July 1955.

10. *Whetstone* 1(2):106-107, Summer 1955.

11. *Cobras and Cockle Shells*, p. 30-31.

12. *Trace* #36:42, Mr/Ap 60.

13. "On Syntax in Poems," pt. 3. *The Blue Guitar* #18, Spring 1961.

14. *Midwest* #2:31-32, Summer 1961.

15. *Poetry* 98(3):198, June 1961.

16. *Nolo Contendere*, p. iii.

17. *New Mexican* (Santa Fe), October 20, 1963.

18. *Latitudes* 1(1), February 1967.

19. Letter to the author, August 2, 1968. In 1968 Smith worked on a book about Crews' poetry, to be entitled *A Cruise with Judson*. It was never published.

20. p. iii.

21. p. iv-v.

22. *Taos News*, July 11, 1991.

23. *The Plastic Tower* #9:39, December 1991.

24. *The Plastic Tower* #8:43, September 1991.

25. For the citations to these reviews, see the Appendix to this book, under "Secondary Sources: Book Reviews."

26. *Atom Mind* 3(11):1, Summer 1993.

27. *Mannequin Anymore That*, p. [0].

28. Unpublished.

29. Unpublished. Burlingame has taught at the University of Texas at El Paso, and has published poetry in many magazines including the *New England Quarterly Saturday Review, Southwest Review, Massachusetts Review, New Mexico Quarterly Review, Poetry Northwest* and *Northwest Review*.

30. *Wormwood Review* 6(1):34-35, 1966.

31. *New Mexican* (Santa Fe), June 27, 1965; reprinted in her *Looking for the Frontier*, p. 34-37. MacNab later published poetry under the names Hava Arden and Arden Tice.

32. Blake and Crews share other common ground, unknown to Foster. In "The Everlasting Gospel" (ca. 1818), Blake wrote:

> Was Jesus Born of a Virgin Pure
> With narrow Soul & looks demure?
> If he intended to take on Sin
> The Mother should an Harlot been.

and in 1991 Crews, who does not remember having read "The Everlasting Gospel":

> This empty shibboleth—God become
> Man. What brag. Had I the power
> to be conceived without sperm, surely
> I'd have had the guts to be born
> not of a virgin—but of a hag

33. *El Crepusculo* (Taos), June-July 1966. Foster, a novelist, was one of the last surviving members of a group of Taos people—Mabel Dodge Lujan, Dorothy Brett, Witter Bynner, Spud Johnson, Andrew Dasburg, and a few others—who were closely associated with D.H. Lawrence.

RESPONSE TO THE CRITICISM

Coffield

In *Criteria for Poetry*, Glen Coffield claims that Crews "has not made a full or resolved use of historical method." He thinks that it should be "more orderly and better resolved." The poetry as reviewed in *A Poet's Breath* represents ideas and symbols which he claims "remain in the slothful disorder of the unconscious." He says that Crews' profundity is made of "random selection, kaleidoscopic accidents," and that Crews is "attached to the affected and the perverse blank page school of art, which based its aesthetics on the sewers of Paris."

Coffield sums up Crews' achievement when viewed from the standpoint of "history" as representing (1) neglect of craft, and (2) "mere dabbling in subject matter." He concludes that "Crews in his present frame of mind, and attitude, is not an artist, but a dilettante," that Crews' philosophy is a borrowed one, and that "he creates unit by unit instead of unit with unit, and his sense of creation does not sufficiently extend to what he is doing with his total production."

The general evaluation of Crews that follows the review of the eighteen poems in *A Poet's Breath* adds little. He elaborates to some extent on what he believes to be Crews' dependency on "other people's ideas." He does admit that the element of "commonality" which Crews draws "from his observation of the South and from his descriptions of boyhood experience" are valid and can provide him "his best opportunity to make a real contribution."

He says that Crews' "use of language is atrocious, really atrocious" and that his poetic techniques "consist of any jingling little metric with big words substituted for the little ones." The creativity of the poetry is said to be "largely reactions (rather than creations) and as such he is a slave to the shortcomings of others." Finally he qualifies the areas Coffield has chosen to examine: "I would suggest that a seventh-grade geography might help to break the monotony of much of his recent work."

A Poet's Breath contains a number of fine poems, including "The Poise of Restless Wonder," "In Artifact," "Slow Cranes on Bold Wings," and "Darling Darling Darling."

The language in "Darling Darling Darling" reveals anything but "a jingling little metric":

> The animals are lowing in sight
> of the gutted glades
>   the gibbeted sparrows
> drift in number above the shallow night
> the castrate wind is rolling down
> and flight is welded to the frosted rim
> of a sky as serene as slumber
>
> The latitudes are wrenched in the ranges
> smothered in spotless resistance
> quenching the questioning passions
> standing as ruthless as callow despair
>
> The decisions are wallowed in mercy
> flowing like the sacred wind
>   the eunuchs
> are cleansed in dispassion and gorged
> on the rinds of their manhood
>
> But the sky is sweeping to solstice
> and the sparrows scream in their terror
> the wind is as ragged as a blind apostle
> and is swept down to the smothered glades

This poem would in itself seem to answer many of Coffield's criticisms. Not only is its language musical, but its rhythm is as deliberate as the weather of the winter in the Rockies of New Mexico.

Furthermore, in almost every line it gives the lie to Coffield's claim that Crews' use of nature is "largely generalities, not fine perception, or considered description." What could be more specific than "the frosted rim of a sky serene as slumber," "the sparrows scream in their terror," "the wind is as ragged as a blind apostle and is swept down to the smothered glades"? Anyone who has spent a fall and winter season in the high Rocky Mountain country of New Mexico and Colorado will recognize the perception and considered description in these lines.

As for the thought, a perceptive reader will recognize the austere and impersonal spirit of the country evoked by the poem. The land itself denies subjectivity. We cannot impose ourselves or our problems upon such a landscape.

The spirit of the poem is the spirit evoked by D.H. Lawrence in his essay "New Mexico," where he described the landscape of Taos:

> It had a splendid silent terror, and a vast far-and-wide magnificence which made it way beyond mere aesthetic appreciation. Never is the light more pure and overweening 2than there, arching with a royalty almost cruel over the hollow, uptilted world.[1]

The technique which Crews has employed in many of these poems may well baffle a formal concept of meaning. In many instances there is a laconic quality to the language. There are meanings cast out, seemingly slow, but which, whip-like, snap the reader back to reality in the "day sense," the literal sense. Against this literal factor is projected the inner reality launched by means of laconic allusion. The subconscious is effectively expressed by this method. A conventional, formalized critical approach will reveal only prose and not poetry.

Coffield has commented on Crews' inability to produce "an original or true insight into the weakness of saints." The validity of Crews' insights into the nature of saints is demonstrated in "Slow Cranes on Bold Wings," also included in *A Poet's Breath*:

> No fiercer pain is bestowed on denial
> than the whisper of love at the farthest nerve
>
> Vines are less tortured by the grapes gone sweet
> than the anchorite emboldened by earnest dread

No wine is so sterile that the winter is wasted
no crevice of longing is spawnless of spore

The winter that strikes the blossomest season
is the one most dreaded for wanton destruction

The bird that pecks dung on the cobblestoned street
is stronger of feather than the loverless night

No stream is so salty from junction to source
that the pussy willows shun the rim of its bank

The bunk of the saint may be coarsened with straw
but the limpingest passion will warm it to down

no night past the feeling feathered in flesh.

This poem presents, in a series of metaphors, the truth of love as it
is expressed in all human life, symbolized in the sexual. It evolves
around the key metaphor of the "anchorite," out of which spring the
thematic variations on the liberating influence of human love, warmly
embodied in sex.

The metaphors that follow the opening statement elaborate it:
"vines," "grapes" and "wine"; "winter," "season," etc.; "the bird pecking
dung on the cobblestoned street," "the loverless night."

The nature of the anchorite or of saints generally is seen to have its
essence in their denial of life. Self-mortification, which has made up
much of the activity of western mystics and saints, has its basis in fear
and frustration. References in the poem point to the possibility that
western mystics might emerge with an affirmation of life. Yet denial,
more often than not, has marked man's self-concern in the role of his
"sainthood." Consecration and dedication have rationalized deeper
motives and deeper needs, which have never been allowed to flower.

Coffield's attempt to evaluate the poetry of Judson Crews is limited
from a number of points of view. In the first place, his use of the
category "History" as a means of opening up or exposing a main trend
in the poet's work is entirely too limiting. History would seem to be

one of the lesser of his preoccupations. Contemporaneity, commonality, language, technique, perception, experience: any of these would
have been far more appropriate. On the other hand, when one surveys
the length, the breadth and the depth of Crews' poetry, one comes to
the conclusion that he is too eclectic, too large a figure, and his thought
and sensibility cover too great an area to be confined to one point of
view, even as an approach.

I liken his work in many ways to that of the painter Picasso. He
has written and experimented in so many mediums. He has grown
from the first attempts at rhymed verse to free verse. He has taken up
the image poem, and emerged from it into a phase of "Gongoristic"
writing, to the kind of poem produced by William Carlos Williams.
From this he has developed also, adding the richness of language,
texture in words and rhythms that we find in Wallace Stevens. He has
continued his own personal development. Throughout all these various
periods his voice has remained his own. He has not, as Coffield claims,
"produced only volume, which is not additive." It is additive in every
sense of the word.

Coffield contradicts himself when he says: "He is perhaps the victim
of his own philosophy, which has never shown signs of being really
his, but is merely borrowed, and so does not apply in any sense," but
then adds: "A single individual cannot construct by his own efforts in
one lifetime what it took the entire race several centuries to put
together." He takes Crews to task for having little respect for tradition,
and as a result suffering the usual penalty of artistic failure.

It is unfortunate that Coffield should have attempted at the time he
did to make a comprehensive critique of Crews' poetry. He did not, I
believe, have much more to work on than fragments, some hurled out
white hot during a time of great change in the poet, when a shift was
taking place in balance and in the use of language itself. In many ways,
the work that Coffield writes about reflects the confusion of the age,
only in this confusion Crews was and is creating, all the while, an
artistic order and unity. It cannot be seen in scattered poems. It can be
seen in poem after poem, through each period: the pattern, the order,
the design, from beginning to what end.

Judson Crews has no respect for tradition when it becomes inhibit-
ing to the creative function. He has no respect for history when that
respect is only a crutch to lean on. He has exposed the language of the

poem to free experimentation in some periods, but it has been an
experimentation with an added strength, the integrating power of the
true artist, who creates a form even out of chaos.

The following poem illustrates something of Crews' understanding
of the power in himself which is the artist:

The Secret Order

To guide the hand
                            among all disorder
to any certain order

The artist speaks
                            against all ages
more certain than stone

The eye of the poet
                            seeded in sorrow
sows acres of light

Even the sword-punctuated
                                        denial of life
flowers to a new flowering

The testament of rebellion
                                        quieting every wound
because we are one

That we are one
                            is the secret order
no disorder may shatter

A Poet's Breath contains nineteen poems—certainly not
representative by any means of the gamut of Judson Crews' poetry.
This however does not constitute my main defense. These poems are
bits protruding, like the tips of icebergs out of the water: fragments
representative and in some cases reminiscent of the poetry written
when Crews first appeared in 1942 with a small pamphlet called *Psalms*

for a Late Season. The language of the poem "Speckled Speckled Dove" reminds us of one of the opening poems in *Psalms for a Late Season*, but it is the relationship of a growing, continuing world, out of the matrix of a language, particular and peculiar to the individuality of the poet:

> For the scalpels are cast in the depth
> and no lifting will restore them to living

Coffield seems to be looking for definite, tangible philosophical meanings. He would project upon the poetry his own compelling need to analyze them as "history," and thus extract from a random selection of nineteen poems a conclusion that they fail historically. He says: "Without historical example the present is likely to seem unimportant or unrealizable, and such example is the more necessary for contrast when new history is being made. Although Crews has not made a full or resolved use of historical method, yet in places he has suggested what his or another's poetry might become, if more orderly and better resolved, and supported by historical example."

To analyze the pamphlet from this point of view is too limited. The history with which Judson Crews is concerned is not chronological. It is not linear. History in the creative sense cannot be anything but subjective. The historical allusions in this man's poetry form only a part of the artistic whole. They are mainly allusory, connotative, suggestive—more in the sense of haiku.

For example, in his poem "Sallow Sallow the Sign Yet Wreathed," such words as "King," "Congo," "Roman," "Tarawa," "Casino" carry us a thousand years or more back in time, and also forward. Here a conception of history in the chronological sense would be violated, but certainly not in the creative, subjective sense. If one has some knowledge of history, it is perfectly clear.

> They came and asked
> then they departed and bound their wounds
> the hero forbade them to sleep on the capitol lawn
> they were asked to return from whence they came
> but how can a man return again to his mother's womb
> when he is old

Here is suggested the war veterans' march on the Capitol to plead for pensions, 1930-31. But the poem only carries the historical continuity in the allusive, connotative sense, which is its structural strength historically.

The last two lines:

> And who ever listens to a thousand years
> who in the midst of even one hundred hungry days

carries us faultlessly from King, Congo, Roman, Washington, to Tarawa, Casino, the naked fact of necessity against a thousand years of history.

Again and again and again we find history in Crews' poems, but this history is always a part of the poem. It serves the uses of the poet.

A New Perspective

Any consideration of Crews' poetry must address the matter of Vers Libre. Even yet in critical or academic circles there seems to be a certain reservation about the free verse, cadence form, despite the revolution in American and modern poetry dating from Whitman and receiving its breakthrough in Pound, the Imagists, William Carlos Williams and most of our modern poetry. The breakthrough is no more clearly apparent than in the work of Judson Crews.

It seems to me that any such reservation represents a cultural lag. To consider the relevance of free verse to metrical verse is tantamount to beating a dead dog.

The poet can no longer count his syllables or his measures on any kind of metrical basis. To retain his full creative flow, he must have access to the form given by the intuitive evolution of a poem from its own intrinsic core of feeling.

It was surprising to read, for instance, of May Sarton, who after years of adherence to meter announced that she has taken up free verse and found it to be just as exhilarating and challenging a discipline.

If Academia thinks it can slow or check an attempt to halt the revolution taking place in language, it is only putting its finger in the dike. All of the technical devices of a language and the prosody peculiar to it are available to the free verse poet. Assonance, consonance, onomatopoeia, caesura, measure in the form of cadence, and yes, even rhyme, are at the poet's hand.

It is simply that in the creation of form, multitudinous and infinite, it allows a greater range and a greater depth than has ever been achieved before.

Whitman said:

> I myself but write one or two indicative words
> for the future.
> I but advance a moment only to wheel and
> hurry back in the darkness.
> I am a man who, sauntering along without
> fully stopping, turns a casual look upon you
> and then averts his face,
> Leaving it to you to prove and define it,
> Expecting the main things from you.[2]

Crews has gone beyond the spare preoccupation with image and being that we find in William Carlos Williams. He has also gone beyond the symbolic complexity and technical effects of Wallace Stevens. The eclectic, colloquial range of Pound's extractions from history and classical literature are matched in the range of Crews' references, richly supplied by all that the modern world has to offer, unprecedented in the complexity and power of its means of communication: radio, television, cinema, and the wealth of publishing, printing machinery and techniques.

The six poems analyzed in Chapter 2 of this book barely scratch the surface of his world.

He cannot be limited to the "Confessional Poem," as written by Robert Lowell, Sylvia Plath, Allen Ginsberg, Roethke, John Berryman or Anne Sexton.

The same holds true of the so-called "Projectionists," such as Robert Creeley, Charles Olson, Robert Duncan and Denise Levertov.

You cannot place him as another Frost, or Stevens, or a Pound or a Jeffers.

We have the "poets of the New Academy," as it is named by M.L. Rosenthal,[3] who include Randall Jarrell, John Ciardi, Winfield

Townley Scott, Richard Eberhart and Karl Shapiro. Rosenthal rather loosely bestowed this name on a group of writers of whom many are connected with the colleges and universities.

If we consider "the poets outside of the Academy," we have in mind such as Kenneth Rexroth, Allen Ginsberg, Charles Olson, Denise Levertov, Paul Blackburn, Robert Duncan, Robert Creeley or Lawrence Ferlinghetti.

Crews is the contemporary of all these poets, appearing in many of the same magazines over the years. He cannot be classified as part of the "New Academy" in the sense Rosenthal defines it. Nor can he, by virtue of the spirit and tradition from which he writes, be placed in any inclusive frame of reference as representing any kind of academic tradition.

He does not represent a school or theory of poetry stemming from the American academic tradition which evolved in the use of formal metrics in a free creative sense, with strong intonations of further-back disciplines gained from a long period of exposure to the English Department classics.

Randall Jarrell delineates to some extent the range of William Carlos Williams' work by saying:

> Williams's imagist-objectivist background and bias have helped his poems by their emphasis on truthfulness, exactness, concrete "presentation"; but they have harmed the poems by their underemphasis on organization, logic, narrative, generalization—and the poems are so short, often, that there isn't time for much.[4]

But one of the particular and peculiar qualities of the poem and of the power of poetry itself lies in brevity, conciseness, exactness, truthfulness. Without these basic elements we do not have poetry.

Two of Crews' poems will serve to illustrate the virtuoso quality of his art. They are in the Williams mode but are undeniably Judson Crews:

Christ Head

Thy straight snozzle
meek and terrible

Formidable as
a ram's prick

Swoon eyed—
I get your point

Castro bearded:
Your meaning is perfect

I shall set
the little chapel

Afire. And watch
the blazes

Here is displayed a masterful use of phrase. One word more or less
could have spoiled it. "Achievement of Love" illustrates again a mastery of the line as phrase revolving around the image of the whole.

Achievement of Love

And how
shall the whale
achieve love

in a storm
of churning

caps, spume
ice blocks flowing

No privacy
of courtship

in the sea

rearing
like a submarine
blasted
from the depths
of a churning
sea

but his mate
abiding

and his penis
man-long
leaping free

and then
go diving

These poems proceed effortlessly, with the same ease with which Williams will, at the right moment, the exact moment, present us with the red wheelbarrow in its unsententious significance.

Crews' poetry has organization, logic, narrative and generalization. It contains "live data," yet this data is extended by the strength of thought, feeling and technique. A mark of great art, great poetry, is this ability to launch into the undefinable and by so doing to create definition.

Many of Crews' poems reveal his narrative, colloquial skill. The living language is given a new form on the page. He tells us in

Narration as Mobile

The thing: the thing: thought is being
though a thousand years hence
speech is pluperfect
                    it moves
faster than sound, faster than action
for it is action accomplished in sublime

The text is motion
and the moral
it existed a thousand years to now be said

The deed will be spoken
the subtle gesture
buried in the confused ganglion
tomorrow
the house tops will ring

and the blind progeny stumbling
why
why, why

Such poems as "Bean Jack the Glore," "The Poise of Restless Wonder," "Stommer Bulltoven Crown," illustrate his narrative ability and his command of the colloquial. They also illustrate the strength of his organization, his logic.

His ability to generalize is represented strongly in "What Babylon Was Built About," "No Father Where the Light Is Shed" and "Delve in the Secret Mind."

Selden Rodman says:

> The tragedy, the unfulfilled renown of our verse,
> is due in no small part to the failure of the poets
> of sensibility to accept that challenge and to the
> followers of Whitman for wrapping themselves in
> his Americanism.[5]

The challenge Rodman refers to is to destroy the validity of Henry James' judgment that the American people would reject Whitman because "it is devoted to refinement."[6]

It is my belief that Judson Crews answers this challenge more completely than any poet thus far. He has met it on more points of reference than any and with greater art.

James Agee's intensity of indignation at the materialism and spiritual poverty of America, reflected likewise in Roethke, Kenneth Rexroth, Byron Vazakas; the simplicity, direction of image devised by

William Carlos Williams; the "social protest" poem as exemplified in Karl Shapiro; the "soul searching" of Robert Lowell's "Confessional poem": all of these strains are to be found in Crews' poetry.

Kenneth Lawrence Beaudoin has referred to "the rugged quality of his verse, the brittle, metallic brilliance of his language." He has defined it as a "suave, urbane language," and has called attention to "his natural rhythms, cultivated modulations, his calculated effects."

Joseph O'Kane Foster has written that "no one since Blake has matched more beautiful rhythms to the spirit's unfolding than Judson Crews." This refers not only to his technical complexity, but to the complexity and depth of his thought. He points out the paradoxes of his "technical virtuosity" and his "plain-spoken artlessness," and the meanings which lay "in his tremendous symbol-ridden world."

G. De Witt arrived at the conclusion that "Deception of Eve" "contains few conceptual impurities and therefore comes close to presenting itself as a single fused image. The full image is released."

Winfield Townley Scott has found his poems "sensual and sensuous, vigorous, quick, and whether the tone is loving or loathing, they may be said to be on the side of life."

Of his use of language, L.W. Michaelson describes the quality of its life: "He likes warm, flesh-bloody words, and uses them well, in fact there's something of the Old Renaissance love of the word here. I mean, Crews does like the sound, the taste, and feel of words, he drives them before his pen with a whip and they bounce, squirm and joggle."

Scott Greer sums up his poetry as being "sophisticated and Gnostic, with a brilliant imagistic surface."

Robert Creeley suggests the dedication and the depth of his work when he says that Crews "asks for nothing and lives sparsely in his work, a place for survival, where the test of a life is that which is possible in it, terrors of image, dreams, sensualities, hard thought, all given place."

The negative side of the appraisals reveals one point of view which is virtually an indictment of his method, his philosophy and his possibility. But Glen Coffield's evaluation addresses only a limited segment of his poetry, and a segment limited to one phase of his writing during an experimental period.

He was more or less summarily dismissed by Hugh Kenner, who however said in conclusion: "Mr. Crews can be an impressively lively writer between asterisks."

John Forbis attempts to impose a limitation on the poet by relegating him to the simple: "Crews, as his better poems prove, is quite at home when he deals with the simple. His long suit as a poet is a knowledge for making the commonplace uncommon, for portraying the unusual with an urgency that is arresting and often a bit terrifying.... When he assumes sophistication, he goes out on a limb...when he attacks themes profound, prophetic, or world-stirring the limb breaks." His review also refers only to a limited segment of Crews' poetry.

It is evident that we have had only a cursory consideration of Judson Crews. He was a contemporary of all the well-known poets of our time, appearing with a steady regularity year in and year out from the mid-1930s until the present time, yet he has been ignored. He has been compelled to bind his own poems, to photo-offset reproductions cut out from the magazines in which he has appeared, and to place them between cardboard covers printed by his own hand, in order to present his work to a limited audience. The record would seem to read something like Whitman's; a printer, publishing his own work. Only Crews has never used a famous name, as Whitman did, to catch a ride to heaven.

This singular integrity and dedication to the work at hand marks Crews not as a recluse, nor an "escapist" from society, but as an original genius whose work will live and be given its due regardless of the auditory difficulties presented in a space age when the ear is assailed by sonic booms, television, radio and super-highways. An age which, by virtue of its materialistic pursuits, screams for law and order and the police when it finds itself at loss in chaos. An age with an auditory mechanism registering computer-like the net results of human activity, and which perhaps somewhere deep within its mechanical realm of wires, gears, and mathematical dials will register the loss that is the voice of the human spirit, sensitive and alive to the world around it.

Such as the world is, at this point, we can only pause and reflect on Walt Whitman's words: "To have great poets we must have great audiences also."

Notes

1. *Phoenix*, p. 143.
2. "Poets to Come." In *Leaves of Grass*, p. 11.
3. *The Modern Poets*, p. 244-264.
4. Introduction to *Selected poems*, p. xv.
5. Introduction to *100 American poems*, p. 26.
6. *The Nation*, November 16, 1865. Reprinted in *Views and Reviews*, p. 101-110, and *The Portable Henry James* (New York, Viking, 1951), p. 426-433.

PART 3

Philosophy and the Poet's Communication

In *Way to Wisdom,* Karl Jaspers says that contemporary philosophy is facing the problem of communication in an age of alienation, when man is isolated from man.

> The basic philosophical attitude of which I am speaking is rooted in distress at the absence of communication, in the drive to authentic communication, and in the possibility of the loving contest which profoundly unites self and self.... The ultimate source is the will to authentic communication, which embraces all the rest. This becomes apparent at the very outset, for does not all philosophy strive for communication, express itself, demand a hearing? And is not its very essence communicability, which is in turn inseparable from truth?
>
> Communication then is the aim of philosophy, and in communication all its other aims are ultimately rooted: awareness of being, illumination through love, attainment of peace.[1]

Other philosophers have come to similar conclusions on the significance of language to the perception of truth. Ludwig Wittgenstein is said by G.J. Warnock to have

> paid more attention than [Bertrand] Russell had done to the ways in which language must be supposed to be related to the world of which we wish to speak, and to the character of the "logical axioms" of which, according to the doctrine, reality was composed.[2]

He reminds us that Wittgenstein speaks of "the bewitchment of our intelligence by means of language,"[3] and insists that our forms of expression prevent us in all sorts of ways from seeing clearly what lies before us.

Whorf

With this in mind, I will consider some concepts involved in the work of Benjamin Lee Whorf, a profound scholar in the science of linguistics. I believe there are concepts shared by Whorf's theories and the poetry of Judson Crews. Crews has never studied these theories; he has only heard of them "at third hand." Of Whorf's conclusions from research on the Hopi Indians Crews wrote:

> There is no doubt a relevance of some of this to some of my work, especially through the image that is not itself because that is exactly what it is (Jaime De Angulo's "Trickster" or the existential Zen).[4]

In his foreword to Whorf's *Language, Thought, and Reality*, Stuart Chase wrote:

> The Greeks took it for granted that back of language was a universal, uncontaminated essence of reason, shared by all men, at least by all thinkers. Words, they believed, were but the medium in which this deeper effulgence found expression. It followed that a line of thought expressed in any language could be translated without loss of meaning into any other language.
>
> This view has persisted for 2500 years, especially in academic groves. Whorf flatly challenges it in his second major hypothesis. "A change in language," he says, "can transform our appreciation of the Cosmos."[5]

Whorf believes that one of the important coming steps for Western knowledge is a re-examination of the linguistic backgrounds of its thinking, and for that matter of all thinking:

> My task is to explain an idea to all those who, if Western culture survives the present welter of barbarism, may be

pushed by events to leadership in reorganizing the whole human future.

This idea is one too drastic to be penned up in a catch phrase. I would rather leave it unnamed. It is the view that a noumenal world—a world of hyperspace, of higher dimensions—awaits discovery by all the sciences, which it will unite and unify, awaits discovery under its first aspect of a realm of *patterned relations*, inconceivably manifold and yet bearing a recognizable affinity to the rich and systematic organization of *language*, including *au fond* mathematics and music, which are ultimately of the same kindred as language. This idea is older than Plato, and at the same time as new as our most revolutionary thinkers. It is implied in Whitehead's world of prehensive aspects, and in relativity physics with its four-dimensional continuum and its Riemann-Christoffel tensor that sums up the *properties of the world* at any point-moment; while one of the most thought-provoking of all modern presentations, and I think the most original, is the *Tertium Organum* of Ouspensky. All that I have to say on the subject that may be new is of the *premonition in language* of the unknown, vaster world—that world of which the physical is but a surface or skin, and yet which we *are in* and *belong to*. For the approach to reality through mathematics, which modern knowledge is beginning to make, is merely the approach through one special case of this relation to language.[6]

Theobald

Whorf does not mention the role of the poet. But there was a lecture by John Theobald, a poet and teacher in San Diego, the contents of which were printed in 1958 under the title, "Language as Living Myth." Theobald's lecture stemmed directly from the theories of Benjamin Lee Whorf. Prefacing the lecture was the following editorial comment by Miles Payne:

There is one group of workers among us not only equipped but charged to initiate a general and continuing movement toward a new reach of awareness, and that is the poets. Their perceptions cut across all nationalism, rigid, jello-mouldy religions, philosophy (poetry is philosophy with wings), and prepare the time and climate for the other arts. Not only new ideas of government and living religion flow from burgeoning awareness but new music and spaces for the plastic arts as well. It is the primary struggle by the poets who join hard conceptual thinking with emotional ecstasy to bring their works into being that establishes the new colony of consciousness where others may follow. It was transportation to such a colony that Longinus had in mind when he said: "The effect of elevated language upon an audience is not persuasion but transport." And it was what Shelley meant when he wrote: "Poets are the unacknowledged legislators of the world."

Unless poets are content to subside in their force as "makers" and abide as mere ciphers in the accounting of society (especially the rage of epidemic bookkeeping, anemic academia division), then the issue of what Benjamin Lee Whorf calls "the significant presentation to consciousness" falls inescapably upon the present parliament of poets and involves the quality of their legislation.[7]

The editorial then quotes Whorf:

So far as we can envision (man's) future, we must envision it in terms of mental growth. We cannot but suppose that the future developments of thinking are of primary importance to the human species. They may even determine the duration of human existence on the planet earth or in the universe. The possibilities open to thinking are the possibilities of recognizing relationships and the discovery of techniques of operating with relationships on the mental or intellectual plane, such as will in turn lead to ever wider and more penetratingly significant systems of relationships. These possibilities are inescapably bound up with systems of linguistic expression.[7]

In "Language as Living Myth," Theobald also refers to Whorf:

> Certain linguistic forms, or "morphemes" as Whorf calls
> them, appear to drop from heaven to express certain truths
> far far in advance of the culture of all the individuals who
> speak that language....
> The formulae held in highest esteem today are mathemat-
> ical formulae, whereas in the past they were poetical form-
> ulae. But mathematics is, after all, a language. What Whorf
> has shown is that the spoken language of tribes toward
> which we thought we could adopt a patronizing attitude (he
> usually appealed to the language of the Hopi Indians, because
> he had studied it most) is found to contain, in its ordinary
> usages, certain highly significant formulations for which no
> individuals belonging to those tribes could possibly be
> responsible. This would account for the fact that certain
> languages can usher us into certain orders of reality, *which
> are there*, but which were not there for us before that reality
> thought fit to co-opt as it were the language necessary to
> express it. That other insurance man, the poet Wallace
> Stevens [Whorf and Stevens both worked for insurance
> companies in Hartford, Conn.], was aiming at this same fact
> when he said, "It is not only that the imagination adheres to
> reality, but, also, that reality adheres to the imagination and
> that the interdependence is essential."[8]

He continues:

> I should like to say that the untranslatability of all true
> poetry is connected with its unique advantage, in that poetry
> exploits unabashedly what Whorf shows to be the disguised
> condition of all language. Poetry unashamedly seeks to attain
> the condition of those other sign languages, Music and Math-
> ematics, where the equivocation between lexation and mor-
> pheme is plainly gone, and the individual elements are
> unmistakably subordinate, entirely taken up into a meaning,
> passion, and radiance not their own (Jesu, joy of man's desir-
> ing...) (or the Mathematical symbol "Pi," meaningless in

itself, but essential to the determination of the area of a circle).[8]

In *Language, Thought, and Reality,* Whorf writes:

> Speech is the best show that man puts on. It is his own "act" on the stage of evolution, in which he comes before the cosmic backdrop and really "does his stuff." But we suspect the watching Gods perceive that the order in which his amazing set of tricks builds up to a great climax has been stolen—from the Universe![9]

He develops the idea, which he says is unfamiliar to our modern world, that other cultures, the Eastern, have recognized a historical continuity much longer than the West. They have recognized that Nature and Language are inwardly kin. He proceeds from the idea of the Indian mantram and mantric art, which in its basic form is an incantation of primitive magic. He claims that in the higher culture they have different, intellectual meanings, dealing with an inner affinity of language and cosmic order. From this point the mantram becomes "Mantra Yoga." It

> becomes a manifold of conscious patterns, contrived to assist the consciousness into the noumenal pattern world—whereupon it "is in the driver's seat." It can then *set* the human organism to transmit, control and amplify a thousandfold forces which that organism normally transmits only at unobservedly low intensities.[10]

Whorf says that we would call this a "Higher Ego." He claims that this trait of the higher ego bearing its resemblance to the personal self organizes itself in language around the three or more pronominal person categories, centered upon the first person singular. At this point he startlingly reveals that any child can learn any language with the same readiness!

He then traces such terms as "name," referring to the lexical level, the phonetic level. Due to the difficulties of supplying exact equivalents from the Sanskrit to our language, such a word as *Manas* is poorly compared to our word "mind." The sense of "the Manasic plane" is a better way of putting it. Another way is to say: "The mind is the slayer of the real," which he quotes from Fritz Kunz, who speaks of *the voice of the silence.*

The Manas level of Hindu thought develops into higher levels called *rūpa* and *Arūpa.* The realm of name and form is *nāma* and *rūpa.* Thus, says Whorf,

> Shape segmentation and vocabulary [are] part of the linguistic order, but a somewhat rudimentary and not self-sufficient part. It depends upon a higher level of organization, the level at which its *combinatory scheme* appears. This is the *Arūpa* level—the pattern world par excellence.... *Arūpa* is a realm of patterns that can be "actualized" in space and time in the materials of lower planes, but are themselves indifferent to space and time. Such patterns are not like the meanings of words, but they are somewhat like the way *meaning appears in sentences* [emphasis mine]. They are not like individual sentences but like *schemes* of sentences and designs of sentence structure. Our personal "minds" can understand such patterns in a limited way by using mathematical or grammatical *formulas* into which words, values, quantities, etc., can be substituted.[11]

It is in these patterns, not stated in mathematical formulas but within the formulas of the poem, that we may find the meanings behind the higher levels of organization of which Whorf speaks. The poets capable of registering them are few, just as there are only a few among the wise men of the East. Walt Whitman's often quoted "To have great poets we must have great audiences also" certainly informs us of the necessity to communicate, of the necessity for language to be elevated, heightened, understood, for communication to reach the higher levels of understanding—as does Wallace Stevens' insight quoted above about the mutual adherence of reality and the imagination.

It is rather astonishing to find that Whorf, who writes at times like an inspired poet, should have been so completely unaware of poetry. He was scientifically educated, oriented, acclimated. He came upon the truth of language. Could he have pursued his quest further before he was cut off, he would eventually have found the poet. He does recognize the limitations of our sciences. He says:

> Science cannot yet understand the transcendental logic of such a state of affairs, for it has not yet freed itself from the illusory necessities of common logic which are only at bottom necessities of grammatical pattern in Western Aryan grammar.... Science, if it survives the impending darkness, will next take up the consideration of linguistic principles and divest itself of these illusory linguistic necessities, too long held to the substance of Reason itself.[12]

He prophesies:

> Western culture has gone farthest here, farthest in determined thoroughness of provisional analysis, and farthest in determination to regard it as final. The commitment to illusion has been sealed in western Indo-European language, and the road out of illusion for the West lies through a wider understanding of language than western Indo-European alone can give. This is the "Mantra Yoga" of the Western consciousness, the next great step, which it is now ready to take. It is probably the most suitable way for Western man to begin that "culture of consciousness" which will lead him to a great illumination.[13]

De Witt

The relationship between the philosophical concepts of Jaspers, the theories of Benjamin Lee Whorf, and the poetry of Judson Crews is to be seen in the remarkable explication by G. De Witt of Crews' poem "Deception of Eve," reproduced in Chapter 4 of this book.

In an introductory article on prosody theories De Witt emphasized "the phrasal significance of the poem." He said that "the poet Judson Crews has established his main metaphor which organizes the whole poem...through a two-part metaphor which presents perceptual relationships which fuse into a single image. *A verbal Ikon founded on the phrase.*"

De Witt quotes three writers on prosody and the meanings in poetry: David Daiches, Josephine Miles, and L.A. Driere. Daiches believes that "the poem depends to the maximum degree on the order of the individual words. The poet arranges the words in such an order that the total complex of meaning is achieved."

Josephine Miles says: "The way a language constructs its sentences is the way it constructs its poem, the characteristic of the sentence giving character to the whole statement." De Witt interprets this as saying that the poet must not only use the clause but also must submit to the clausal constructs characteristic of the language.

L.A. Driere, on the other hand, asserts: "For poetic construction... there is...the negative principle of avoiding or diminishing the effects usually obtained by the prose construct." De Witt suggests that, in contrast with Miles, both Daiches and Driere imply that the syntax of a successful poem differs from that of a non-poem.

De Witt concludes:

> In other words the poem rises from its syntax.... If great danger lies in the habit of the reader to view the poem as a non-poem— a container for propositions—and if the poem rises from its syntax, the poet must ask which structure does more to move the poem away from the propositional fallacy. And the answer is clearly that the phrase is more appropriate than the clause, the characteristic syntax vehicle for non-poems.[14]

Meanings leap out from De Witt's explanations. The method of the poet bears uncanny resemblances to the language and thought constructions which Whorf projects. Only this is not from the world of science. It is not the language of mathematics but the language of the poem.

De Witt continues by saying that

> clauses run to rhetoric, phrases to the esthetic.... Imagery is perceptual, and the phrase remains with percept; the clause, on the other hand, moves to concept.[15]

He concludes that few purely phrasal poems exist, and the reason is that most poets are not theorists.

> They do not recognize the phrase as their great ally because they have never thought clearly, if at all, about the epistemological dangers of the clause.... They are, like everyone else, culturally conditioned. They write poems; therefore they use words, and they use the words as the culture as a whole employs them—in clauses.... We are arguing here for the thesis that, whatever the majority practice, the ideal poem is phrasal and that "successful" clausal poems tend to be those with substantives powerful enough to snap the harness of their syntax.[16]

It is in the use of the phrase that Judson Crews excels. De Witt contends in his explication of "Deception of Eve" that

> The phrasal structures...release the full image.... The poem contains very few conceptual impurities and therefore comes very close to presenting itself as a single, fused image.... The success of this organic poem rests at least in part upon its syntax.[17]

Whorf approached the study of language as a scientist. This was his orientation. He did indicate the significance of other modes of approach when he said:

> Language has further significance in other psychological factors on a different level from modern linguistic approach but of importance in music, poetry, literary style, and Eastern mantram.[18]

The significance of language as represented in the poet is the key to the riddle presented by Whorf.

In the beginning the philosopher was poet.

Crews

In an introductory article for the only issue of his magazine *Poetry Taos*, Crews wrote:

> Beauty is manifold and any soul that sees it has dropped a few curtains from before his self-censured sight. Once having seen it, it is easier to see it again. An Artist's vision grows even as a mystic's. And once he is fully grown his vision will encompass the world.
>
> For surely as Tao is known to the Tibetan monks so is poetry the first key to religious enlightenment. And the two in time and place may become as water in motion of light at twilight through aspen's autumn leaves...or dawn ...or the rose.
>
> Maritain posited finally that there are but two ways to knowledge, the way of the saint and the way of the sinner. But the sinner's search may lead to sainthood, whereas the saint is a sinner still if he needs to search at all.[19]

Forsaking Abstraction

The meditation of the man as man
is another thing than man as poet
another thing than either poet-man
or than man-poet

The meditation on night
is another thing than night
and meditation on man
is a meditation too frightening
for either man-poet or man

All past ages are in man
all past meditations are in
the ultimate meditation
but the ultimate meditation
is neither in man nor man-poet

> The ultimate meditation
> for all past ages and past meditations
> for all these men and poet-men
> the ultimate meditation will be
> not of the night, but in the night

In an essay on the work of a New Mexican Spanish-American wood carver, Patrocinio Barela, he said:

> Death, for Jean Cocteau (and for many of us), is perfectly symbolized in a beautiful princess. But in a subsistence culture, where the struggle is for survival of the very physical body, it is not surprising that the symbol of the middle ages, bleached bones in a black shroud, is still the most potent.
>
> Nor does this posit an absence of spiritual values. Quite the contrary. The death of the soul is a problem facing primarily the effete, the well washed and well fed. The man living close to physical destruction has faith and is strong, or he lacks faith and is a coward.[20]

He considers the matter of art:

> And here we come to the crux of the matter, art has no certain content. The content is drawn from the soul of the beholder. And this content is not static as long as the soul is alive. It is not static, even for the artist himself.
>
> No piece of art is a record of all that the artist has intended. No piece of art is a record of a one sure thing. A piece of art that can be comprehended by any human being, including the artist himself, is a failure.
>
> A blue print can be read to the last detail. But a piece of art cannot be finally read until the last man is dead and God is dead also.[21]

Conclusion

The poet's vision is important to philosophical thinking. The processes by which man grows towards achieving philosophical being, as indicated by Karl Jaspers, are the processes which the true poet and artist go through in order to achieve their being in the creative: the phases of wonder, doubt, the sense of forsakenness, the upheaval; the wonder leading to knowledge, the doubt leading to certainty, the sense of forsakenness leading to the self. These developments within the soul are known by the poets. Jaspers then says that these are not enough, these three motives are not adequate. He says, "They can operate only if there is *communication among men.*" It is here that the poet finds his real being. The poet must communicate. If he is a poet of great depth such as Judson Crews, he operates from firm foundations, from a depth of being achieved by the power of the inner creative drive.

Such a poet, such a man has the awareness of being, has found the illumination of love, and has attained a state of inner peace achieved only by a rare few. He has acquired the requisites which Jaspers believes are necessary for the fulfillment of man's philosophical being. He has, by virtue of the inner disciplines afforded him by his wrestle with the meanings of his art, achieved a state of being. When we consider Jaspers' statement,

> In man's domination of nature there remains an element of
> the incalculable which represents a constant threat, and the
> end is always failure: hard labour, old age, sickness and
> death cannot be done away with,[22]

we know we are in the realm of the poet's reference. Life.

Notes

1. *Way to Wisdom*, p. 26-27.
2. *English Philosophy since 1900*, p. 49.
3. *Ibid*, p. 55.
4. Letter to the author, August 31, 1968.
5. *Language, Thought, and Reality*, p. vii.

6. *Ibid.*, p. 247-248.

7. Payne, Miles. "A letter to the Parliament of Poets." *The Light Year*, Autumn 1958.

8. *The Light Year*, Autumn 1958.

9. *Language, Thought, and Reality*, p. 249.

10. *Ibid.*, p. 249.

11. *Ibid.*, p. 253.

12. *Ibid.*, p. 269-270.

13. *Ibid.*, p. 263.

14. "On Syntax in Poems," pt. 1. In *Blue Guitar*, #18, Spring 1961.

15. *Ibid.*, pt. 1.

16. *Ibid.*, pt. 1.

17. *Ibid.*, pt. 3.

18. *Language, Thought, and Reality*, p. 266.

19. *Poetry Taos.*

20. *Patrocinio Barela*, p. 9.

21. *Ibid.*, p. 10.

22. *Way to Wisdom*, p. 21.

Epilogue

In 1942, when Judson C. Crews published his first slender volume of poetry, he was a clean-cut young man right out of Yoknapatawpha County. Not exactly that county, but surely that country close to the piney woods of East Texas and Louisiana, along the Brazos River where Waco lies, and where also lies Baylor University, fount of Educational Baptism.

Waco was also the home of William Cowper Brann, the publisher of a paper called *The Iconoclast*. Brann was to confront controversial issues of the day with a disconcerting lack of fear of opposing public opinion. He was shot in the back, just where his suspenders crossed, on a certain day in April 1898. (Nicknames for Waco in those last years before the turn of the century were Athens of the West and Six-Shooter Junction.) Brann had whirled around and shot his enemy full face forwards, not once but several times, until his fingers could no longer hold his revolver. Both men died as a result of the encounter. Brann's tombstone to this day stands in the cemetery at Waco with a piece chipped out of it by the bullet of another enemy who hated him for his fame and his too free speech.

Out of this fast-waning frontier came Judson Crews. Like Brann, he has always been willing to take on all comers who would deny him the right of free speech. His poems speak of men and women, their penises and their vaginas, their cocks and their cunts. He leaves us no hole to crawl into, to hide in when writing of men and women and human desire, of longing and lust. He only knows that along the way of life most of us are cheated. Sold short on our longings. Sold short on love by the crippling inhibitions of organized society.

If we follow him from the mid-1930s to the early 1990s, we see his constant involvement with speech, and the meanings whereby speech is augmented in the poem. Like the prose of William Faulkner, his poems abound in vigorous and measured language. They take their form out of the sound of language itself as it is spoken with an intensity rendered only in poetry.

In spiral fashion his art has grown from year to year. Sometimes a kind of rhetoric takes over, an involvement with Freudian references, symbols right out of totem and tabu. Hardly ever Jung, that maker of myths. Not Crews, who would never burden those kites he sent up for all to see with a leaden anchor of illusion dangling from them. Language and language alone would carry his poems and the substance of their meanings.

American meanings. Search through every chapbook over those years and you will find within the strata of his language many meanings pertinent to our time and our place. They extend beyond the border of the conscious mind. They embody that umbilical area wherein lie our dreams, our nightmares, our aspirations and our fears.

Crews revealed his lifelong preoccupation with language in his first book, *Psalms for a Late Season*. The Psalms are lyrical and loving, with a brevity of delivery and poetic form. They display also his concern, reflecting the dark years of the Great Depression, for the deprived status of the laboring force of humankind.

Titles of his chapbooks suggest speech: *You Don't Have To, You Can See Why, Politely Suggest, The Difference Between, The Lives You Should.* The substance with which he deals is revealed in other titles: *The Feel of Sun and Air Upon Her Body, The Heart in Naked Hunger, The Wrath Wrenched Splendor of Love, To Wed Beneath the Sun, More Love of....* Their meanings and their language engage us. First our attention, then our comprehension. They all revolve, a kind of Bachian fugue, an interwoven intricacy of form and language. He can play endlessly on these chords.

Yet in his later years he sought, searched for and found his way again in poems outspoken and brief. Suggestive and blunt too in many of their meanings. Brevity would characterize his growth and development over the years, despite the rare deviation to long poems such as *Nations and Peoples* and *Dolores Herrera.*

He has also moved away from the complexity and the witty word combinations for which he was sometimes known in the 1950s and 1960s. Many of the poems of that period were rich in metaphors, some of which I have attempted to explicate in this book. Traces of these elements may still be found in the later work, which however tends to be more simple, direct, even conversational.

He has always written about love and sex. His later preoccupation with the interrelationship of man and woman has been a theme since the beginning, though the expression has become more explicit with the years.

Now he stands alone. All by himself, so to speak, naked as a jay-bird and all the more formidable as a poet for the exercise of his language, his speech and the meanings he wishes to give us.

They become various styles: psalms in praise of love or life, elegies or mocking commentaries on contemporary life. They reveal a gamut of emotions ranging on a keyboard so very rich in meanings and tones. A polychrome as it were of love and of life. All we ask at this point is to hear more of his men and his women, and of life ever-abundant even in its anguish and its joy.

Works Consulted

The reader is also directed to the "Secondary Sources" section of the Bibliography in the following Appendix.

Abbe, George. *You and Contemporary Poetry.* Peterborough, N.H.: R.R. Smith, 1965.

Allen, Donald M. *The New American Poetry, 1945-1960.* New York: Grove Press, 1960.

Brinnin, John Malcolm. *William Carlos Williams.* Minneapolis: University of Minnesota Press, 1963. (*Pamphlets on American Writers,* #24)

Brooks, Cleanth, & Robert Penn Warren. *Understanding Poetry.* 4th ed. New York: Holt, Rinehart and Winston, 1976.

Ciardi, John. *How Does A Poem Mean?* 2nd ed. Boston: Houghton Mifflin, 1975.

Coffield, Glen. *Criteria for Poetry.* Eagle Creek, OR: The Author, 1954.

Contemporary American Poetry, comp. D. Hall. Harmondsworth, Eng., Baltimore: Penguin Books, 1971.

Drew, Elizabeth, George Connor. *Discovering Modern Poetry.* New York: Holt, Rinehart and Winston, 1961.

Drew, Elizabeth. *Poetry: a Modern Guide to Its Understanding and Enjoyment.* New York: Norton, 1959.

Eckman, Frederick. *Cobras and Cockle Shells: modes in recent poetry.* West Lafayette, IN: Sparrow Magazine, 1958. (Vagrom chap book, #5)

Fifteen Modern American Poets, comp. G.P. Elliott. New York: Holt, Rinehart and Winston, 1956.

James, Henry. *Views and Reviews.* Boston: Ball, 1908.

Jaspers, Karl. *Way to Wisdom: an Introduction to Philosophy.* New Haven: Yale University Press, 1954.

Lawrence, D.H. *Phoenix: the Posthumous Papers of D.H. Lawrence,* ed. E.D. McDonald. London: Heinemann, 1936.

Lawrence, D.H. *Selected Poems.* (Introduction by Kenneth Rexroth.) New York, Viking Press, 1959.

Major American Poets, ed. O. Williams & E. Honig. Mentor Books, 1962.

Miller, J. Hillis. *William Carlos Williams: A Collection of Critical Essays.* Englewood Cliffs, NJ: Prentice-Hall, 1966.

100 Modern Poems, comp. S. Rodman. New York: New American Library, 1949.

100 American Poems, comp. S. Rodman. 1st Penguin Signet Books ed. New York: New American Library, 1948.

Parkinson, Thomas. *A Casebook on the Beat.* New York: Crowell, 1961.

Payne, Miles. "A Letter to the Parliament of Poets." In *Light Year,* Autumn 1958.

Poet's Choice. comp. P. Engle & J. Langland. New York: Dell, 1962.

Pound, Ezra. *Selected Poems.* New ed. New York: New Directions, 1957.

Rexroth, Kenneth. *Assays.* Norfolk, CT: New Directions, 1961.

Richards, I.A. *Practical Criticism: a Study of Literary Judgment.* New York: Harcount, Brace and World, [1963?]

Rosenthal, M.L. *The New Poets; American and British poetry since World War II.* New York: Oxford University Press, 1967.

Rosenthal, M.L. *The Modern Poets: a Critical Introduction.* New York: Oxford University Press, 1960.

Stevens, Wallace. *Poems.* (Introd. by Samuel French Morse.) New York: Vintage Books, 1959.

Theobald, John. "Language as the Living Myth." In *Light Year,* Autumn 1958.

Tindall, William York. *Wallace Stevens.* Minneapolis: University of Minnesota Press, 1961. (Pamphlets on American Writers, #11)

Untermeyer, Louis. *Modern American Poetry.* New & enl. ed. New York: Harcourt, Brace & World, 1962.

Warnock, G.J. *English Philosophy since 1900.* 2d ed. London, New York: Oxford University Press, 1969.

Whitman, Walt. *Leaves of Grass.* Garden City, N.Y.: Doubleday, c1926.

Whorf, Benjamin Lee. *Language, Thought, and Reality.* 1st paperback ed. Cambridge: M.I.T. Press, 1964.

Williams, William Carlos. "Kenneth Lawrence Beaudoin." In *Inferno,* #6 & #7, 1952.

Williams, William Carlos. *Selected Poems.* Introd. by Randall Jarrell. Enlarged ed. New York: New Directions, 1968.

APPENDIX

A Bibliography of Judson Crews

by Jefferson P. Selth

Acknowledgments

A background of librarianship, though invaluable to a researcher, does not exempt him from dependence on other librarians and their assistants. Those whom I have particularly to thank are Lila Blinco, in the Special Collections Department at the University of California, San Diego, who invariably responded to my many phone calls with speed as well as thoroughness; Janet Steins of SUNY-Stony Brook, whose experience of both research and the New York Public Library were enthusiastically placed at my disposal; Gladys Murphy at the University of California, Riverside; and Elizabeth Burns, Cynthia Kimball and Mike Basinski of SUNY-Buffalo's Poetry-Rare Books Collection. Although I knew Buffalo's treasury of small-press poetry was the nation's finest, I still underestimated its wealth and allowed too little time there; had it not been for the enthusiastic cooperation of these lovers of poetry, I would have had to return at considerable cost in time and money. This book owes much to them.

J.P.S.

ABBREVIATIONS

Pseudonyms, etc., used by Judson Crews

[C.F.]	Cerise Farallon
[G.]	Greasybear
[T.D.]	Trumbull Drachler
[W.E.B.]	Willard Emory Betis

Books

AA	Alphabet Anthology
AAW	Against All Wounds
AFTT	Angels Fall, They are Towers
AP	The Anatomy of Proserpine
AT	African Transcripts
BDS	Blood Devisable by Sand
CCM	Come Curse to the Moon
CLA	City Lights Anthology
CM	The Clock of Moss
CYAM	Can Your Ass Over Mudge
DB	The Difference Between
DHNP	Dolores Herrera/Nations and Peoples
DRA	Desert Review Anthology
E	Eropoesia
FSAB	The Feel of Sun & Air upon her Body
GMV	Gross Mother of Verse
GDD	A Good Day to Die
HD	Holy Doors
HF	Honeymoon Fwimming
HNH	The Heart in Naked Hunger
HO	Hica Osit
HPH	Hermes Past the Hour
HSA	Hampden-Sydney Anthology
I	Incognito (= *Guts* #6)
IBG	Inwade to Briney Garth

145

IH	Itable in Her
II	If I (= *Wormwood Rev* #83)
LBL	Live Black Lusaka
LYS	The Lives You Should
MAT	Mannequin Anymore That
MC	More Crews
MHC	Mehy in his Carriage
MLM	More Love of ... More & & &
MOS	Modern Onions and Sociology
MS	Marriage Skins [*MS* is also a magazine]
N	The Noose
NC	Nolo Contendere
NDCN	Never will Dan cause no one to
NN	No is the Night
NP	Nations and Peoples/Dolores Herrera
OMWF	Once More with Feeling
OWH	The Ogres who were his Henchmen
P	Poems (1978)
PB	A Poet's Breath
PLS	Psalms for a Late Season
PSW	Poems Southwest
RFA	Roma a Fat at
S	Symbiosis
SCA	Second Coming Anthology
SH	A Short to Holy
SK	The Stones of Konarak
SP	Selected Poems
T	Travois
TDV	To a Dead Vehicle
TH	Trojan Horses
THYM	To Help You Man
TM	Three on a Match
TWBS	To Wed Beneath the Sun
UTEV	An Uninhibited Treasury of Erotic Verse
UWNB	A Unicorn when Needs be
VA	Voices from Africa
VB	Ver Batim
VRG	Voices from the Rio Grande
WWAY	Why We Ask You to
WWCD	What We Could Do

WWSL	The Wrath Wrenched Splendor of Love
WYTC	What You Too can Do to and
YCSW	You Can See Why
YDHT	You Don't Have to
YMAN	You, Mark Antony, Navigator upon the Nile

Magazines

Amer	American
Anth	Anthology
Chbk	Chapbook
Chr	Chronicle
J	Journal
Lit	Literature
Mag	Magazine
Nl	Newsletter
NM	New Mexico
NY	New York
Po	Poetry
Q	Quarterly
Rev	Review

Miscellaneous

arr.	arranged
At	Autumn
Fa	Fall
P.	Press
p.p.	privately printed
pubd.	published
Pubns.	Publications
Recdgs.	Recordings
reptd.	reprinted
rev.	revised, reviewed
Sp	Spring
Su	Summer
tr.	transcribed
Wi	Winter

Only the last two digits of the date of the publication are given, and all refer to the 20th century. Thus 46 = 1946.

Many typographical and spelling errors occur in the poems as printed. This bibliography uses the correct spelling, and refers from that which appears in the book or magazine.

PRIMARY SOURCES

Journals Edited

The quotations are from a letter of Crews to the editor.

Vers libre: a magazine of free verse. v.1-2(4) 36-38. "Every two months was the intent."
Motive. Waco. "1939 or 1940."
Readers Choice. 46-? "A book sales magazine."
The Flying Fish. Taos. #1-4 48 (MEL)
Suck-egg Mule. Ranches of Taos. #1-5 51-52 (MEL).
Taos. Taos. 51. "Concurrently (I think) with *Suck-egg mule.*"
The Deer and Dachshund. Ranches of Taos. #1-6 Sp 51-54. "Begun I think before *Suck-egg Mule* was finished."
The Naked Ear. Taos. "#1-11 Wi 56-Ja 59. Irregular."
Poetry Taos. Ranches of Taos. #1 57 (MEL).

Books

The following imprints are all Crews': Motive Press, Este Es Press, Namaste Press; and all those asterisked (*), which were small (5½" x 4¼") photocopied editions of 3-25 copies.

A Sheaf of Christmas Verse. Washington, D.C.: Three Hands P., n.d.
    (Reprint of the Crews poems in *Three hands*, #4.)
Psalms for a Late Season. New Orleans: Iconograph P., 42.
The Southern Temper. Waco, Tex.: Motive, 46. 32 p.
No is the Night. Taos: Motive Book Shop, 49.
A Poet's Breath. Ranches of Taos, NM: Motive Book Shop, c50.

Come Curse to the Moon. Taos: p.p., 54.
The Anatomy of Proserpine. Ranches of Taos: p.p., 55.
Patrocinio Barela: Taos Wood Carver (with Wendell B. Anderson &
   Mildred Crews). Taos: p.p., 55. Rev. ed.: Taos Recdgs. & Pubns., 62.
The Wrath Wrenched Splendor of Love. Ranches of Taos: p.p., 56. [On
   t.p.: ... *splenbor* ...]
The Heart in Naked Hunger. Taos: Motive Book Shop, 58.
The Ogres who were his Henchmen: Poems. Eureka, CA: Hearse P., 58.
   [On t.p.: *The Orges* ... , an error of the cover artist]
To Wed Beneath the Sun. Taos: p.p., 58?
Inwade to Briney Garth. Taos: Este Es P., c60.
The Feel of Sun & Air upon her Body. Eureka, CA: Hearse P., 60.
A Unicorn when Needs be. Taos: Este Es P., 63; reptd. by Vergin P., El
   Paso, c91.
Hermes Past the Hour. Taos: Este Es P., c63.
Selected Poems. Cleveland: Renegade P., 64.
You, Mark Antony, Navigator upon the Nile. Taos: p.p., 64.
Angels Fall, They are Towers: Poems. Taos: Este Es P., 65.
Three on a Match: Wendell B. Anderson, Cerise Farallon, Judson Crews.
   Taos: Este Es P., 66.
The Stones of Konarak. Santa Fe: American Poet P., 66.
Mehy in his Carriage, ed. Robert Williams Austin. N.p.: Summit P., 68.
Nations and Peoples. Cherry Valley, N.Y.: Cherry Valley
   Editions, 76; reptd. 1991 with *Dolores Herrera* (see below).
Poems. N.p., 78.
Nolo Contendere. Pref. by Robert Creeley. Illus. by Lori Felton.
   Houston: Wings P., 78.
*More Love of...More & & &. N.p.: Amalgamated Distribution
   Enterprises, 78?
*The Difference Between, by Cerise Farallon, pseud. Albuq.: Vaginal
   Vingtetun Editions, 78?
*Honeymoon Fwimming. Albuq.: Tap-water Springs Editions, 78?
*The Lives you Should. Albuq.: Modern Gander Wing Editions, 78?
*Marriage Skins. Albuq.: Gyro-dinner Dumpling Editions, 78?
African Transcripts. (Poems tr. & arr. by JC.) N.p., 79?
Voices from Africa. (Poems tr. & arr. by JC.) N.p., 79?
Live Black Lusaka. (Poems tr. & arr. by JC.) N.p., 79?
*Sting Intere. Albuq.: Teocalli Tadpole Editions, 79?
Gluons, Q. Albuq.: Namaste P., 79?
*Itable in Her. Albuq.: Wholly Ghost P., 79?

You Don't Have to. Albuq.: Amalgamated Distribution Enterprises, 79?

You can See Why. Albuq.: Mid-night Donkey-angel Editions, 79?

A Short to Holy. Albuq.: Laid-back Boomerang Editions, 79?

Politely Suggest. Albuq.: Hard-up Whenever Pubns., 79?

Never will Dan Cause No One to. Albuq.: Holy Terrible Editions, 79?

Yester Dream Portraits of Cutting. Albuq.: Nicodemus Crocodile Pubns., 79?

Roma a Fat at. Albuq.: Instantaneous Centipede Pubns., 79?

Modern Onions and Sociology. Albuq.: Saint Valentine P., 79?

Ver Batim. Albuq.: Whirlpool Reverberations Verlag, 79?

Why we Ask You to. Albuq.: Apple-whetted Contrition P., 79?

What You Too can Do to and. Albuq.: Cartweheel Encounter Pubns., 79?

Songs, by Charley John Greasybear. ("Poems selected and edited by Judson Crews and A. Thomas Trusky.") Boise: Ahsahta P., 79.

The Noose: a Retrospective—4 Decades. Placitas, NM: Duende/Tooth of Time Pubns., c80.

To Help You Man. Ranches of Taos: Motive Bookshop, c81.

Can Your Ass over Mudge. Albuq.: Namaste P., c81.

More Crews. Albuq.: Buckwalter Circumnavigation Editions, 82.

More Men. Albuq.: Spoon-spun Terrigenous P., 82.

The Clock of Moss. Boise: Ahsahta P., 83.

Hica Osit. Albuq.: Suck-egg Mule, c85.

To a Dead Vehicle. Albuq.: Namaste P., c86.

Against All Wounds. Parkdale, Ore.: Trout Creek P., 87. (Backpocket poets, BPS 2)

Gross Mother of Verse. Albuq.: Suck-egg Mule, c88.

Trojan Horses. San Francisco: Incendiary Pubns., c89.

Symbiosis. Chicago: Oyster Pubns./New Romantic Pubns., 90.

Dolores Herrera/Nations and Peoples. Las Cruces, NM: Buzzard's Roost P., 91.

Blood Devisable by Sand. Las Cruces, NM: Buzzard's Roost P., 91.

Mannequin Anymore That. Albuq.: Zerx P., 93.

Poems

Ancestral [T.D.]. *Deer and Dachshund* Sp 51
Ancient of days. *Open cell* 2(1)/#17:5 73
And all the perpetrated delicacies. *CCM; Simbolica* #3 [51?]
And starvation stalking the gold streets. *Crescendo* [1(4)]:11 Sp [42]
And too, sublime. *UWNB; Cresset* 25(1):13 Nv 61
Angel bannered. *Simbolica* #27:31 [62]
Angels and growing. *Simbolica* #18 [59?]
Angle, The. *S*
Another poet down the river, they said. *MAT*
Answered prayer. [C.F.] *Naked Ear* #2 [57?]
Antigone. *Approach* #5:16 49
Antigone. *PB*
Any old time. *AFTT; Harlequin* 1(1):3 Sp 64
Anyone would admit it was a propitiously. *Aura* #25:88 Wi 88
Ape weather. *Odyssey* 1(3):9 59
Apostrophe to the bitch, our pay. *AP*
Apostrophe to the canine. *S*
Apostrophe [C.F.]. *Deer and Dachshund* 1(2) [52?]
Apple doon forthright. *Window* #6:3 53
Appurtenance to a bright. *New Writing from Zambia* 10(3):2 Oc 74
April and spring time. *Blue Grass* #2:24 Wi 63
Aquacade. *UWNB; Inland* 4(1):23 At 60
Arcade, an alcove---light filled, An. *Gypsy* #14 90
Archaic garden (in my, An. *Cafe Rev* 3(7/8):18 Jl/Ag 92
Arching grossness of uncut stems is, An. *Wormwood Rev* 26(3):84 86
Arguments I have made for, The. BDS; *Paper Radio* 8(1) Ap 90
Arrested immolation. *Curled Wire Chr* 2(4):8 Ja/Fe 55
Artist, The. *P; TWBS; Po* 88(1):17 Ap 56
As a bit of. *N; Jeopardy* 8:139 72
As a river facing dusk. *Pig in a Pamphlet* #10 85
As furtiveness, as time. *FSAB; HNH; N; P; Experiment* 6(4) 53
As if a. *Purr* #4 76
As if all /The forked. *Coldspring J* #8:16 Se 75
As if /the blood-lit. *Wormwood Rev* 31(4):130 91
As it was /I slapped. *SK*
As knotty a question. *Wormwood Rev* 15(2):60 75
As simple as your grace is upon. *Plastic Tower* #7:18 Je 91
As that woman /heifer hungry. *Bold Print* [Se 92?]

As time passes. *Wormwood Rev* 13(4):157 73
As you /fondled my cock. *Wormwood Rev* 13(4):157 73
Ascent without contrition. *IBG; Wwhimsy* Su 56
Ash, The. *N*
Ash in. *Wildflower* #3 Mr 82
Asinine observance, An. *Wormwood Rev* 5(3):18 65
Aspersion. *YMAN*
Asphodel's rebuttal, The. *OWH; Gryphon* #1:11 [50?]
Assuming. *Wormwood Rev* 20(4):127 80
Assumption, The. *Iconograph* #2(23) Su 46
At Christmas time. *UWNB*
At crestfall. *Star-web Paper* #6:32 77
At fifty-four. *Smudge* #4:56 Wi 79
At less the rainbird in his reeds. *SCV; WWSL; Three Hands* #4 52
At the tobacconist. *Wormwood Rev* 8(3):31 68
At this moment. *Plumbers Ink* 2(2):51 79
Atoll. *CCM; HPH; Epos* 2(2):[16] Wi 50
Atom bomb cathedral, The. *Climax* #1:35 Mr 55
Attempting to turn tide on a covenant. *TH*
Aubade. *N; New Writing from Zambia* 10(1):7 Mr 74
Augur; the times. *Bozart-Westminster* Wi 41/42
Autumnal dithyramb. *Symptom* Ap 66
Avocado, An. *Star-web Paper* #6:3 77
Babe innocent. *YMAN; Element* 1(1) 60
Back to Jack, back to Jack—this was. *GDD*
Back-lighted. *BDS; Puerto del Sol* v16:19 Sp 81
Bailey I put. *N; Wormwood Rev* 11(3):114 71
Bale of brine the quaver reaching, The. *HPH; Epos* 2(3):11 Sp 51
Bale thaw. *FSAB; Interim* 1(4) 45
Barber's apprentice, The. *Grande Ronde Rev* 2(1):22 67
Barrage, The. *Span* Ju/Jl 41
Basking in the certainty of shadows. *Curled Wire Chr* 2(3):9 Nv 54
Bathroom door being locked, The. *SP*
Battle was never an allure of time. *Blamk Gun Silencer* #5:8 92
Be comforted. *Egg/Surfside Po Rev* 1(2):2 Sp 73
Bead, you say, of the blue wick. *Purr* #5 76
Bean Jack the glore. *AP; CYAM; FSAB; HO; SCV; THYM; Three Hands*
    #4 52

Beast is not its cunning but its brawn, The. *Howling Mantra* 91
Beautiful, plump. *Washington Rev* 5(5) Fb/Mr 80
Beauty. *HPH; Westminster* 45(4):7 Wi 55/56
Becalmed in a carnal dread. *AP; SCV; Three Hands* #4 52
Because of /the horse races. *Wormwood Rev* 7(3/4):36 67
Because you /have hidden. *Wormwood Rev* 15(2):70 75
Bedizened. *NN; Experiment* 4(1) Wi 48
Being a past master-builder of Trojan. *TH*
Being sufficiently fortified. *FSAB; HNH; N; Westminster* 42(3):2 At 52
Being thankless. *Wormwood Rev* 4(1):25 64
Belle, A. *Wormwood Rev* 21(3):51 81
Benadam hick pat. *From a Window* #3 Oc 65
Bending /over. *Z Miscellaneous* 3(2):56 Su 89
Bereft of candor. *HNH; Free Lance* 3(1):20 1st ½ 55
Bike tyre. *Wine Rings* 1(5):3 76
Billy Cod. *Wind* 4(14):10 74
Birth from tears. *Crescendo* [1(4)]:8 Sp [42]
Birth of Venus, The [C.F.]. *Free Lance* 3(1):10 55
Bitchin' brags. *Stone drum* 2(1):8 Sp 89
Bivouac of WACS---that was the haunting, A. *Guts* #6 89
Black art. *IBG*
Black female *Casaba* #3:49 Je 73
Black piety. *NC*
Black sash was all she had. Okay, A. *Lactuca* #12:38 Fe 89
Blinded. *Wind* 10(36):9 80
Blood devisable by sand---isn't it soon. *BDS; Interim* 8(1):40 Sp 89
Blood on our hands. *Grist* 1(4) De 64
Blood-soaked, The. *MC*
Blue behind, The. *Star-web Paper* #6:32 77
Blue concerto, A. *HPH; P; PB; Experiment* 4(3) Su 49
Blue hyacinth, pale blue hyacinth. *N; Gale* 1(8):12 Se 49
Bold as a /python. *T*
Bones of my ribs are misshapen, The. *CM; Cache Rev* 2(1)/#3(5) 84
Born-a-liar Bulltoven. *N; Goodly Co.* #2:18 Ap 64
Bound [C.F.]. *DB; TM; Olivant Q* 1(2):60 4th q 53
Boy, A. *Elizabeth* #13:25 Jl 69
Brain powder and. *Giants Play Well in the Drizzle* #26:4 Jl 90
Break-, The. *McLean County Po Rev* 2(1):8 Fa 76/Wi 77

Bridal path, The. *Wild Dog* #2:8 Ap 63
Bride, The. *Wisconsin Rev* 7(1):25 Fa 71
Bride to my [C.F.]. *DB; TM; Neo.* Fa 53
Bright little masters, The. *HPH*
Brighter places—that's the ex-. *CM; Star-web Paper* #8:9 84
Bringers of death. *UWNB; Olivant Q* [#2]:55 4th q 53
Brink. *Bozart-Westminster* Su 37
Broken esplanade. *CCM*
Buck ass on the town. *Head* #2 65
Buck rail to numbers. *Earthjoy* #2 72
Bulltoven among the thorns. *AP; N; Sheaf* #1:5 Ja 55
Bulltoven crown. *YDHT*
Bulltoven drunk, imagine, on two. *Random Weirdness* #6:23 My 85
Bulltoven once. *Wormwood Rev* 15(2):2 75
Bulltoven said. *Minotaur* #4:33 80
Bulltoven's other brother. *Goodly Co.* #4:4 De 65
Bully the cad. *Window* #8:34 55
Burden grown, The. *TM; South Dakota Rev* 4(1):63 Sp 66
Burial at sea, A. *Mati* #4:57 Wi/Sp 77
Burnished bronze. *Purr* #5 76
Burst forth. *Intrepid* #7 Mr 67
Burst of prey. *YMAN; Poet & Critic* File#2:19 Ap 62
But we could speak to. *See:* Untitled poem /But we could speak to
Butt like a barracuda—small choice, A. *MAT*
By the dead. *BDS; Descant* 30(1):30 Fa/Wi 85/86
By your knees. *Back Door* 1(2):10 70
Cacophony, A. *CCM*
Cadence in ochre. *TWBS*
Cadence of doubt, The. *CCM; Bridge* 1(11) [47?]
Caged. *Aldebaran Rev* #11:17 71
Cain motionless on a high plateau. *CCM; Suck-egg Mule* #1 [51?]
Cain: my brother. *See:* Cain motionless on a high plateau; For the deed
  in the asking
Calculation, The. *Centering* #2 [73?]
Calico foot stool. *HO; CYAM; THYM; UWNB*
Cambrian dusk should evoke some, The. *Pembroke Mag* #22:49 90
Can you /imagine two. *Wormwood Rev* 21(3):60 81
Cane, A. *T*

Cane and his brother, Apple. MHC
Cannibals, The. *YCSW*
Canonical. *Intrepid #7* Mr 67
Canticle lucid and sparse. *HPH*
Capital. *MHC*
Capricious home land. *AFTT; Neon #4*:32 59
Carmeth full refell. *IBG*
Carnation suggesting your bruised, A *Lost and Found Times #25* De
    89
Cart rechant the ransom clere. *HPH; Signet* 3(9):3 Oc 61
Carter crest when the stars are dim [T.D.]. *Struggle* 1(2) Mr 54
Castramentation at the end of battle. *GMV; Lucky Star* 2(3):33 Oc 85
Castrating mothers, castrating women. *Shockbox #4*:21 92
Casuals of war in a city that's never been bombed. *Circle* 1(3):42 44
Cat came back. Whatever was it, The. *Gypsy #21/22* Fa 93/Wi 94
Catacombs. Where no one seems to be, A. *Die Young #6*:7 Su 93
Catastrophe of my genes—conceived, The. *Ash #9*:10 Wi 92
Cats all day. *Wormwood Rev* 15(2):59 75
Cattle the meadows spread. *PB; Po* 75(3):47 De 49
Caught for. *Casaba #3*:48 Je 73
Celestial freeway. *Arx* 2(1):35 My 68
Cerebration. *TM*
Cerrus dawn the rain of frailty. *IBG*
Certain kind of lying, not altogether, A. *S*
Chaos. *Pan American Rev #1*:46 Wi 70/71
Chased by a creature great as the mind's. *AAW*
Cheap, A. *Wormwood Rev* 21(3):[88] 81
Cheek pressing. *Wind* 4(14):10 74
Cherubs and gargoyles are cast down. *Experiment in Words* 3(9):13 92
Childbirth. What do the scriptures really. *CM*
Children dancing. *Madrona* 3(8):28 74
Chokecherry bounce she made, great clusters. *TH*
Choosing /your face. *Kindred Spirit* 7(3):7 Wi 88/89
Christ head. *N; YMAN*
Chromatic simplification, A. *TWBS; Beloit Po J* 1(3):10 Sp 51
Circumambulation. *IBG*
Citadel of breathless wonder. *SP*
Cities of men, The. *WWSL; Cresset* 18(3):15 Ja 55

Classic in the daemoned service. *Zahir* 1(4/5):48 72
Classic mask, male, A. *Star-web Paper* #6:31 77
Clemency [C.F.]. *DB*
Cliffs, The. *YDHT*
Climbing the wall, before the wall climbs. *Po Motel* #4:14 85
Climbing /to the petroglyphs over shale. *CM; N; PSW*
Clock of moss or else a compass, The. *CM; Po Now* #38:9 83
Close /Anima speaks. *Star-web Paper* #6:31 77
Clue of the motionless gander, The. *From a Window* #3 Oct 65
Coast at clear. *Wild Dog* #2:9 Ap 63
Coast, The. *YMAN; Pig in a Pamphlet* #10 85
Cock, The. *Wormwood Rev* 22(4):146 82
Cock of crowing. *See:* Poem—Cock of crowing
Cold for night and lasting. *IBG; Also* #2:57 Sp 51
Cold tree effect, The. *UWNB; Carolina Q* 14(3):61 Su 62
Collage you tossed together like, A. *GMV; Writers Forum* 13 87
Collonials, The. *See:* The Colonials
Colonials, The. *YMAN*
Coloration of an apocalypse, The. *YMAN*
Come down. *S*
Come May. *Purr* #5 76
Come sum Sue Missy. *AP*
Coming to a boil [T.D.]. *Quagga* 1(3):9 60
Committed. *Stone* 3(1/2):11 Su 70
Commode's weather, The. *Desperado* #5 Ju 71
Common quarrel, A. *Wormwood Rev* 21(3):74 81
Complexion of triumph, The. *FSAB; Grecourt Rev* 2(2):119 Fe 59
Complexity of time as it ticks, The. *Ash* #5:10 Fa 90
Composed. *Cache Rev* 2(1)/#3:5 84
Concerning abstraction. *YMAN*
Concerning less of the sea. *N; P; PB; Po* 75(3):146 De 49
Concerning particulars. *DRA; YMAN*
Concession Pilate never made, The. *N; WWSL; Po* 76(3):133-4 Je 50
Confectioner's afternoon, A. *CCM*
Confessions. *BDS; Open 24 Hours* #7 91
Confusion to confusion. *YMAN; Simbolica* #3 [51?]
Conjunctions the dead converge, The. *GMV; Writers Forum* 12 86
Conned out. *Wormwood Rev* 15(2):66 75

Danielle may wring. *TDV; Icarus* p19 Sp 83
Daphne. *HPH; Imagi* 4(1):10 Sp 48
Darkness of some uncommitted frag-, The. *TH; Impetus* #21:7 Ja 93
Darling darling darling. *FSAB; HNH; OWH; PB; Experiment* 4(1):237
     Wi 48
Day time or two. *Jeopardy* 5:110 69
Day's cock of morning, The. *CM*
Dear empire smelling fair. *HPH; N; Miscellaneous Man* #3:8 Wi 54
Dear Harry. *CYAM; HO; T; THYM*
Dear M_____. *TWBS; WWSL; Imagi* 5(2):12 50
Death on a stricken field. *HPH; NM Q Rev* 16(2):211 Su 46
Death. *Gale* 1(8):13 Se 49
Deception of Eve. *Blue Guitar* #18 Sp 61
Declaration at forty. *IRG; N; UTEV; Simbolica* #17:16 [58?]
Dedication. *Crescendo* [1(4)]:10 Sp [42]
Definite and certain and. *OWH*
Definitive, The. *Washington Rev* 5(5) Fe/Mr 80
Deity. *HNH*
Delays that dimmed the lights out, The. *Wormwood Rev* 25(3) 85
Delicate reprisal, The. *Po Nl (Albuq.)* #1 Nv 64
Delineation. *Wormwood Rev* 8(3):31 68
Delve in the secret mind. *CCM; FSAB; Simbolica* #4 [51?]
Departure, The. *HNH; OWH; Crescendo* 2(3/4):20 Wi/Sp 43
Deployed down. *Blackbird Circle* #4:14 Sp 73
Descent into the depths would have changed, A. *Lactuca* #12:37 Fe 89
Desnuda. *AFTT; N; Massachusetts Rev* 4(4):784 Su 63
Desolate condor. *YMAN; Golden Goose* 4(5):9 [53?]
Detailing. *El coqui* #2:33 Ta 78
Devil the level loose wind. *Spearhead* 2(2):23 Sp 51
Devils may whistle God's love. *FSAB; Flame* 6(1):14 Sp 59
Dewey hinterland, The. *Free Lance* 7(1):10 63
Diana assaulted. *HPH; Impetus (Deland, FL)* #7:20 Sp 63
Diary: Homestead widow. *Sanskaras* 1(3):110 69
Did ever /such as I. *Wormwood Rev* 5(3):20 65
Did love fail. *Purr* #3 75
Diety. *See:* Deity
Digging. *MOS*
Din hearth stem as velvet I hold. *Signet* 3(6):9 Je 61

Dreams that the bottom drops out of. *My Legacy* #11C:56 93
Drifting Lou wide haine. *AP*
Drink of forgetting, The. *Tanager* Ju. 43
Driven a fart in the wind. *FSAB; HNH; OWH; Miscellaneous Man* #3:8
    Wi 54
Dromedary soulful beast, The. *AP; Deer and Dachshund* #4 [53?]
Dumb, dear. *Wormwood Rev* 20(4):128 80
Dutch night song. *Pan American Rev* #1:45 Wi 70/71
Dynamics of strategy, The. *PB; TM; Po NY* #1:13 49
Ear, An. *Wisconsin Rev* 7(1):*25 Fa 71
Early bird. *Wormwood Rev* 5(3):14 65
Earth matters. *Bartleby's Rev* #3:2 73
Ease of love when all the moves and, The. *Guts* #6 89
Easier. *Another Chicago Mag* #5 80
Easter suite. *See:* Let's get; Reaching; So squalling; We grew
Econdom eccle haine. *Sheaf* #2:15 Nv 55
Economical, An. *BDS; Egg/Surfside Po Rev* 1(2):2 Sp 73
Edge, The. *Wormwood Rev* 21(3):53 81
Expanse of emptiness looking much, An. *AAW*
Eggs were nesting, The. *Flame* 1(2):5 Su 54
Elegy. *Iconograph* #4:6 41
Elegy upon the death of Martin, An. *N; Po Venture* 4(1):40 Fa 71
Elpinore's overland putsch. *AP; CYAM; HNH; HO; Merlin* 2(3):159
    Su/At 54
Embankment, The. *PSW*
Embroidered, or perchance tattooed. *Wormwood Rev* 31(4):121 91
Emily Dickinson's quaint, stark rhymes. *Wormwood Rev* 31(4):123 91
Empire [W.E.B.]. *Naked Ear* #8 [58?]
End of war, The. *Span* Wi 46/47
Enraptured nude. *Wormwood Rev* 15(2):66 75
Enshrouded in a vapor thick enough. *Po Peddler* 1(4):10 Je 89
Entropy. *Miscellaneous Man* #1:20 Ap 54
Epi-gratis. *Wormwood Rev* 15(2):59 75
Epigram /Wisdom [C.F.]. *Suck-egg Mule* #1 [51?]
Epithalamium. *DRA; YMAN*
Epithalmia. *See:* Epithalamium
Equestrian. *IBG; Contact* 1(2):2 Mr 52
Escutcheon, The. *Micromegas* 1(3):27 Wi 66

Essence. *N; Intrepid* #6 66
Etching, An. *Fault* #14 Nv 79
Eternal phantom of the fever feigned. *Gale* 2(4):7 My/Je 50
Eulogy to a C.O. taken to jail. *Westminster* 36(2):11 Su 47
Evaporation. *Jacaranda* #6:7 Fe 66
Even if /you hurry. *Goodly Co.* #10:16 Nv 67
Even in dreams my life is not with-. *GMV; Pig in a Pamphlet* #10 85
Even /tol ick. *Wormwood Rev* 21(3):82 81
Every dog has his day. *Ms* Jl/Ag. 41
Every electrical. *Wormwood Rev* 15(2):61 75
Everything that [C.F.]. *DB; TM; Curled Wire Chr* 2(5):7 Fe/Mr 55
Examining. *Wormwood Rev* 15(2):68 75
Excelsior. *HNH; Po* 91(4):240 Ja 58
Exile, The. *S*
Exit, The. *Intrepid* #18/19:31 71
Extramontane. *HPH; Berkeley* #9:2 [50?]
Eye teeth. *NDCN; Premiere* #7:6 69
Eyes that. *Zahir* 1(4/5):49 72
Fable. *UWNB*
Fair thoughtful be good. *Hearse* #6:18 59
Fall is with us. *Wormwood Rev* 5(3):20 65
Fallow deer beside us, The. *TWBS; Shenandoah* 2(3):18 Wi 51
Falter not dream. *CYAM; THYM; UWNB; Epos* 3(2):5 Wi 51
Famous poets I have known---. *S*
Fast legs, The. *Margarine Maypole* #42 [79?]
Faster than sound. *Grundtvig Rev and Almanac* #1:23 Sp 50
Fat young, A. *Wormwood Rev* 21(3):70 81
Father, father, the name of sorrow. *See:* Pastoral /Father, father
Fear may be an entity. *Flame* 2(2):6 Su 55
Feather duster, A. *Wormwood Rev* 5(3):15 65
Feathered in spring. *Wanderlust* 1(4):27 Ja 59
Fell theorum. *Essence* #5 [53?]
Female. *OWH; Whetstone (Philad.)* 1(1):7 Sp 55
Few leaves, A. *South Florida Po J* 1(3):75 Sp 69
Fiesta brava. *N; Goodly Co.* #10:17 Nv 67
Figment for faith, A. *FSAB; HPH; Death* 1(1) Su 46
Filial piety. *YMAN*
Finally /I. *NC*

Finding /a con-. *Pinchpenny* 83
Fire flies in slumber. *Bridge* 2(10) [48?]
Fire, The. *Green Horse for Po* 1(2):35 73
Fire-side song [G.]. *Black Bear Rev* 1(3):58 Fa 75
First love. [T.D.] *Naked Ear* #4 [57?]
First tree of autumn. *FSAB; N; P; Black Mountain Rev* #7:188 Ag 57
Five whores in three windows in a. *MAT*
Flared. *Erratica* 1(3):3 72
Flatus. *Dreams & Nightmares* #35:16 Se 91
Flaunting eagles, I beseech you. *Camels Coming* #1 Ag 65
Floating plaza, The. *Goliards* #5:30 Jl 65
Flock. *Toothpaste* #5 71
Floor level, The. *Wormwood Rev* 15(2):70 75
Flower, The. *Purr* #4 76
Flower lathed for metaphored tribute. *MHC*
Flower skin. *Wildflower* #57 Oc 89
Flowers. *Wormwood Rev* 20(4):127 80
Flying. *Road Apple Rev* 1(4)/2(1):5. Wi 69/Sp 70
Foliage of bird, The. *HPH; P; Po Book Mag* 2(2):15 Wi 50
For any possible lover. *HPH*
For Delalia [T.D.]. *Deer and Dachshund* 1(2) [52?]
For elephant bamboo. *Lost & Found Times* #12 Oc 82
For many /years. *Foxfire* 3(3):39 Wi 69
For nameless ever. *Gale* 1(1):6 Ap 49
For neither can we leap. *SP*
For nought the welling past. *AFTT*
For phantom search. *Nimrod* 2(2):9 Wi 58
For plight in catastrophic mull. *Bridge* 6(1):21 Ja 52
For shame in the shadows of trees. *Intrepid* #18/19:33 71
For specific reasons [T.D.]. *Signet* 3(9):11 Oc 61
For the deed in the asking. *IBG; CCM; Suck-egg Mule* #1 [51?]
For the hundredth. *Stoney Lonesome* #4:21 74
For who would climb mountains. *Gale* 1(1):6 Ap 49
Forced march. *TWBS*
Forest arbour you have forfeited, The. *Galley Sail Rev* Ser2(27):41 Sp 87
Forfeit. *NN; NM Q Rev* 16(3):351-2 At 46
Forsaking abstraction. *N; NN; Interim.* 2(3/4):46 46

Forth wing from the feather bird. *Neo* Fa 53
Fortification, A. *Wild Dog* #4:23 Jl 63
Fortuitous answers. *YMAN*
Four fingers are missing. *Boss* #5:70 79
Fragment on a long way come. *Bozart-Westminster* Su 38
Fragmentation. *YMAN; Inferno* #5:22 51
Freak, The. *NC*
Friend of forty years. *CM; Writers Forum* 9:202 83
Friends. *Wisconsin Rev* 5(2):10 Wi 70
Fright of the vine, The. *IBG; Simbolica* #5 [51?]
From an old farmer. *Illuminations* #1:3 Su 65
From the Virgin Islands. *N; Wormwood Rev* 5(3):14 65
From youth. *Out of Sight* 1(1):25 66
Frost, The. *Wormwood Rev* 21(3):57 81
Fruit juice. *Sum* #2:9 Fe 64
Full naked and carnal [C.F.]. *Existaria* #8c:9 Se/Oc 57
Gain spate coxey. *Experiment* 5(3) Fa 50
Game. *Shore rev* #10:10 73
Garden, The. *YMAN*
Garden scene [T.D.]. *Gryphon* #1:14 Sp 50
Gestation. *Ms* #8:[5]. Su/At 42
Girl from home, The [T.D.]. *Sheaf* #2:6 Nv 55
Girl /I liked, A. *Po Now* 6(1):40 81
Girl with /a cockleburr, A. *MAT; Scree* #2 74
Gloria's belly-button was not quite. *TH*
Gloss, A. *Wormwood Rev* 21(3):85 81
God and the devil, why. *Wormwood Rev* 24(2):72 84
God made chickens and children. *Wind* 17(61):23 87
God nebulum miro. *Ab Intra* #1:22 72
God, the idiotic plaints. *CM*
Godden Beach to Warren Mack. *AP; Four Winds* #4 Wi 53
Goddesses. *Desperado* #7 72
Godiva started out. *Blind Horse Rev* #1:27 Jl 92
Golden cage, The. *IBG*
Golden showers. *Experiment in Words* 3(9):13 92
Good /time, The. *Wormwood Rev* 27(4):93 87
Goofing out, turning away---is that. *Wormwood Rev* 31(4):122 91
Great wheels, The. *S*

Greed of my cock---is there any, The. *Paper Radio* 8(1) Ap 90
Green canyon, The. *AP*
Green charioteer, The. *OWH*
Green leather, green leather. *Wisconsin Rev* 10(4):31 Se 75
Gross mother of verse. *GMV*
Growing out. *Wormwood Rev* 21(3):68 81
Gull is by the sea, The. *HPH; N; Path of Beauty* Ag 38
Gut-nut, Lawrence's shibboleth, The. *TH*
Haggard recalculations. *Bridge* 4(9):279 Je 50
Hagiography of a beam of light, The. *Innisfree Mag* 11(7):15 92
Haiku /Last night at midnight. *TM*
Half past seven o'clock. *Head #2* 65
Hard times. *Wormwood Rev* 13(2):71 73
Harlot, A. [W.E.B.] *Naked Ear #4* [57?]
Harshness of the eye's center which is, The. *Raw Bone #7* 86
Harvesting of grain, The. *WWSL; Po Book Mag* 6(3):8 Sp 54
Has it been a game of mine to memorialize. *Shockbox* 1(7/8):10 93
Hasp. *Toothpaste #5* 71
Hate of the joyed young kill, The. *AFTT; Fiddlehead #57* Su 63
Have the hares. *SK*
Have you /heard about it---. *Po Now* 7(2):9 83
Having commandeered my ass and my. *TH*
He left his "ugly thing" pickled in. *TDV; Pig in a Pamphlet #10* 85
He was drunk. Not on. *CM; Po Now* 7(2):9 83
He was likely enough a cadaver for an old. *Ash #5*:18 Fa 90
He was walking sideways on one leg. *CM*
Heart a flower opening like a wound, The. *AP; N*
Heart-shaped face she had but her heart was a, A. *AP; Sheaf* #1:7 Ja 55
Helen again. *Arx* 2(4):44 Ag 68
Hell song [C.F.]. *SScribe* p49 [57?]
Helmets. *Zahir* 2(2):53 76
Hematite ocelot crouches for her killing, The. *Flame* 2(4):4 Wi 55
Hemingway said, I wonder if. *Po Now* 6(6):3 82
Her /beautiful. *Po Now* 6(6):2 82
Her child's. *Santa Fe Po #2*:11 Sp 82
Her conception of the future was spiked. *My Legacy* #11C:65 93
Her /consciousness. *Lake Superior Rev* 9(2):17 Wi 78
Her cunt had more in common with. *Pearl* #13:58 Sp/Su 91

Her eyes are. *Surfside Po Rev/Egg* #4:44 Wi 73
Her hands. *Wormwood Rev* 21(3):55 81
Her nakedness in. *NC*
Her nakedness reaching. *Earthjoy* #2 72
Her nightgown sometimes trailed after her. *My Legacy* #11B:17 93
Her pants were not tight but so slim-. *AAW*
Her purse in. *Ab Intra* #1:22 72
Her round /buttocks are. *SK*
Her thoughts are other than my own. *MAT*
Heralded Helen she came. *IBG; Simbolica* #14 [55?]
Heraldry. *IBG; Literary Calendar* p12 Su 56
Here is the island, fishy enough. *AAW*
Here the longing whisper. *HNH; Kansas Mag* p26 56
Here we plotted. *Wisconsin Rev* 6(3):15 Su 71
Hermit's /tabernacle, The. *Wormwood Rev* 21(3):73 81
Hermit's throne, The. *Free Lance* 3(1):19 1st ½ 55
Hesperides. *Head* #2 65
Hey-do hey-do. *CCM; HNH; Glass Hill* #3 Mr 50
Hidden dream masqueraded by, The. *BDS; GMV; Interim* 6(2):24 Fa 87
Hide the leap of the roe. *P; UWNB; Descant* 4(3) Sp 60
High line skeeter. *Coffin* #1 [65?].
Hijo de algo. *IBG; N; Contact* 1(2):1 Mr 52
Hint of the rotten core, A. *Ms* My 41
His hat was on straight as he approached. *CM*
Hobert said. *Wormwood Rev* 11(3):114 71
Holed up three days. *Wormwood Rev* 15(2):63 75
Holocaust. *Arx* #10:50 Fe 68
Homage to Melpomene. *IBG; Bridge* 3(6) Ja 49
Home again of noname beginning, The. *Pearl* #14(30) Fa/Wi 91
Honey dripping in the comb. *FSAB; HNH; Imagi* 5(2):12 50
Honing. *Wildflower* #2 De 81
Hope scape bish-bop. *Intrepid* #7 Mr 67
Horse with the cockleburs in its fetlocks, The. *Wild Dog* #11:13 Oc 64
Horses. *Margarine Maypole* #41 [79?]
Horses whose hooves never slashed. *BDS; OMWF*
"Hot days there have been" in various hells. *Guts* #6 89
Hot image, A. *Arts in Society* 4:2 Su 67
Hot lonesome and loose as. *HNH; TWBS; Olivant* Q [2]:54 4th q 53

Hotel where we had two beds, both of them, The. *TH*
House, The. *Happiness Holding Tank #3/4* 72
How bright the morning sun is, penetrating. *CM*
How can it be that my sexual imagery. *BDS; Pembroke Mag #22:49* 90
How clearly we entered the forest. *CM*
How could she, loathing her own guts. *Kindred Spirit* 7(3):7 Wi 88/89
How did /you ever know. *Wormwood Rev* 21(3):56 81
How exquisite I thought Ed Corbet's. *Lactuca #14:37* My 91
How fast. *Wildflower #37* Je 4 86
How happy the precocious crab. *PB; Retort* 4(2):12 48
How long, how long. *OWH; Death* 1(1) Su 46
How many bright, darting. *Po Now* 7(2):9 83
How many crushed skulls they found. *CM; Atom Mind* 3(11):61 Su 93
How many generations of pusillan-. *Ash #9:10* Wi 92
How many /times. *Bonesauce #11:13* [89?]
How much /it's going. *Wormwood Rev* 21(3):66 81
How much the world has. *BDS; Dog River Rev* 10(2):25 Fa/Wi 91
How often /I fuck my poems. *Goodly Co. #15* Ap 70
How often I used silence to mask anger. *Chiron Rev* 12(1):11 Sp 93
How quickly and quietly. *Blind Horse Rev #1:26* Jl 92
How quietly /does the human. *Folio* 5(1):5 Wi 69
How round. *Paper bag* 2(2):28 Sp 90
How the constants change--weathered. *Coventry Reader* 4(1) Sp 91
How to pace the return back from no-. *Tandava* v14:14 My 88
How vehemently contemporary editors. *S*
How warmly. *Ash #9:29* Wi 92
How white /the bride is. *Star-web Paper #6:31* 77
How womanly. *Cache Rev* 2(1):5 84
Humans were her appurtenances. *GMV; Blue Light Rev #9:18* Wi 87/88
Hunting season. *N; YMAN; Unusual* 1(3):30 55
Hure Cassie Gotwid. *AP; Sheaf #1* Ja 55
Hymen. *Happiness Holding Tank #10* 73
Hymn /The distilled attar. *AFTT; Crescendo* 2(3/4):20 Wi/Sp 43
Hyperbole. *CYAM; HNH; HO; THYM; Curled Wire Chr* 2(6):11
    Ap/My 55
I always liked tall girls---even in Africa. *Wormwood Rev* 27(4):92 87
I am [C.F.]. *Naked Ear #7* [58?]
I am /accused of. *NC; Po Now #26:22* 80

I am aware /D.L... *San Marcos Rev* 2(2):45 At 79
I am eternally fallen between two stools. *BDS; Pembroke Mag* #19 87
I am I because my little dog knows. *TH*
I am not as philosophical about. *Free lunch* #12:9 Su 93
I am not logical, and I am not reason-. *Pig in a Pamphlet* #10 85
I am still as stone. *BDS; Po Now* 6(6):3 82
I applied. *NC*
I ask /of the hero. *NDCN*
I awake. *Wind* 4(14):10 74
I awoke with. *Pig in a Pamphlet* #10 85
I called you Maurice because. *Sub Rosa* #27:20 Oc 88
I came back to that same desolate place. *TDV; Po Now* 6(6):3 82
I can not. *Wormwood Rev* 15(2):64 75
I conceded hours and days---night time. *Impetus* #9:57 Fe 87
I could smell her ass or else. *MAT*
I defy you. *Po Now* 5(3):30 80
I denied the destiny of gender---denied it. *Wormwood Rev* 27(4):92 87
I dented. *Wormwood Rev* 21(3):80 81
I did not /walk away from. *Abraxas* #27/28:23 83
I didn't have to practice hold-. *MAT*
I didn't /let you. *GMV*
I didn't set. *NC*
I do not /mind. *Happiness Holding Tank* #10 73
I do not want to say that our seven. *Old Red Kimono* p58 Sp 87
I don't know whethe[r] she believed it. *S*
I don't want /to make pretty poems. *Wisconsin Rev* 10(4):32 Se 75
I emptied. *River Rat Rev* #4:19 88
I fought pitched battles with three. *MAT*
I fucked /her. *NC*
I fucked her first in the kibbutz. *Impetus* #13:28 Fe 88
I get /drunk. *NC*
I got some /blank enunciations. *Toad Hiway* #3:3 Je 90
I had never observed horses before, really. *Pig in a Pamphlet* #10 85
I had seen her enough. *GMV; TDV; Galley Sail Rev* Ser2(24):31 Sp 86
I had sized. *Wormwood Rev* 21(3):78 81
I had thought of this camp-out engage-. *Wormwood Rev* 26(3):83 86
I hardly struggled at all before. *MAT*
I have a fantasy act going on in. *TH*

I have a screen door now that I can. *MAT*
I have cut myself apart in several. *Wormwood Rev* 27(4):93 87
I have described. *Scree #3* 75
I have driven. *Wind* 4(14):11 74
I have kept walking sometimes, walking in place. *MAT*
I have never been much of a moun-. *Open 24 Hours* #5:66 86
I have not /climbed. *NC*
I have not /crossed my. *McLean County Po Rev* 2(1):8 Fa 76/Wi 77
I have not named anything its name. *Wormwood Rev* 24(1):10 84
I have /ordered my being. *Howling Mantra* 91
I have sat /on my ass. *N; From a Window* #3 Oc 65
I have shut. *N; Wisconsin Rev* 9(4):25 [75]
I have trashed all closest-of-kin. *GMV; Poetpourri* 1(4):20 De 87
I haven't spoken *N; Wormwood Rev* 15(2):67 75
I knew /empirically. *NC*
I knew /the sound well. *Pinchpenny* p27 82
I learned the two-line stanza. *TDV; Planet Detroit Mag* #6:15 Su 85
I left them. *Look Quick* #10:10 Sp 82
I lied. *Wormwood Rev* 27(4):93 87
I lighted a fire. *Wormwood Rev* 5(3):15 65
I like /that girl. *Wormwood Rev* 21(3):86 81
I love Jane. *Wormwood Rev* 13(4):156 73
I never /choose. *Guts* #6 89
I never listened closely enough to. *GMV; Stone Drum* 1(6):19 Sp 88
I never /make a big. *Wormwood Rev* 21(3):70 81
I once did a hilariously funny. *Wormwood Rev* 25(3) 85
I open my mouth and it is a vast cave. *Guts* #6 89
I parked that damn girl's Cadillac. *Chiron Rev* 12(1):11 Sp 93
I read /your erotic poem. *NC*
I remember mud in an ancient time. *Art Mag* #6 86
I sat down in that great blonde chair. *GMV; Amelia* #9:49 87
I should not /have returned. *Wormwood Rev* 15(2):69 75
I simply love that girl Kate—. *Alchemy* 28:59 93
I sleep crazy hours. I take crazy. *Blank Gun Silencer* #6:26 Sp 93
I told you that I told you. *Wisconsin Rev* 5(2):10 Wi 70
I too /would cry out. *Atom Mind* 1(4):15 Sp 69
I used to /make. *Wormwood Rev* 21(3):83 81
I wanted even. *Zahir* 1(4/5):49 72

I was all ready to say on a general im-. *BDS*
I was less blackmailed by your words than. *Reflektion* #9 Nv/De [90]
I was never feverish except maybe to con-. *Guts* #6 89
I was not freaked out by her. *TDV; Pig in a Pamphlet* #10 85
I was out-manoeuvred from the start. *Chiron Rev* 11(1):2 Sp 92
I was writing /haiku. *Outcast* #4 67
I went /to get *Wormwood Rev* 21(3):71 81
I who terribly demand the naked. *AAW*
I will not /gainsay. *Dragonfly* 4(1):47 Ap 73
I will not profane God. *Grimoire* #5:41 Su 83
I won't /predict. *Quixote* 5(4):28 69
I won't try. *NC*
I won't /waste breath again. *Wormwood Rev* 21(3):59 81
I would moan the shit out of my. *Blank Gun Silencer* #7:46 93
I wouldn't think /of writing. *NC*
I'd have twisted. *SK*
I'd trade it. *Poetpourri* 2(2):19 Su 88
I'll feed cats no more milk at my own. *Guts* #6 89
I'll fuck you. *SK*
I'll make /my bed. *Howling Mantra* 91
I'll not cop out on rhododendrons this. *Wormwood Rev* 24(2):72 84
I'll put it /to use. *Wormwood Rev* 21(3):56 81
I'm tiring of this broken. *See:* Poem—I'm tiring of this broken land
I've been known /for a. *N; T; Tawté* p21 My 75
I've been /thinking. *Pembroke Mag* #7:108 76
I've ex-. *Wormwood Rev* 24(1):10 84
I've lost all terror of a junta, left or. *Bonesauce* #11:11 [89?]
I've never won a prize and wouldn't. *BDS*
I've not /found. *McLean County Po Rev* 2(1):8 Fa 76/Wi 77
I've not /turned my back on. *Wine Rings* 1(5):2 76
I've seen worse, as they say, without even. *Lactuca* #12:39 Fe 89
Idea /of not getting, The. *Lactuca* #14(38) My 91
If a Mazda lamp. *TDV; Another Chicago Mag* #9 83
If a poem /were made. *Wormwood Rev* 21(3):65 81
If a stone were your forfeit. *Folio* 6(1):36 Su 70
If a woman, a particular woman. *Conditioned Response* #6:14 [87?]
If any sculptor. *Nausea One* 1(3):7 Su 73
If belief. *Bleb* #6 Nv 72

If Bulltoven liked those girlie-butt. *BDS; Atom Mind* 3(11):64 Su 93
If Bulltoven's reputation got worse yet. *Wormwood Rev* 26(3):85 86
If but for the queen. *Jacaranda* #6:7 Fe 66
If eternity is patient to reinvest all its holdings. *Art Mag* #6 86
If God /had devised. *Wormwood Rev* 7(3/4):36 67
If God's pain exceeds. *Cafe Review* 3(7/8):18 Jl/Ag 92
If going to bed would help anything. *MAT*
If he swam at all it was in a religion. *Lactuca* #12:38 Fe 89
If I am where. *Stone Country* 74(2):16 My 74
If I assumed sex should come first. First. *Gypsy* #14 90
If I begin a poem with "if," where. *Guts* #6 89
If I could photograph a blowing. *Blind Horse Rev* #2:4 Ja/Fe 93
If I could think of a story with a diff-. *Blue Light Rev* #6:14 Su 86
If I /escaped. *This is Important* #11 85
If I had been horse-whipped a few times. *Cehsoikoe* #8 Ap 89
If I had gone quietly into the hills. *CM*
If I had /my skin. *Wormwood Rev* 20(4):126 80
If I /had not hacked. *Wormwood Rev* 21(3):[49] 81
If I had sorted out all the quietness. *CM*
If I had sorted out all. *HO; Beloit Po J* 33(3):7 Sp 83
If I had /worn out. *NC*
If I had your "monkey" on a stick, what. *MAT*
If I have known testaments of the great---. *Thunder Sandwich* #4 85
If I have not praised. *UWNB*
If I have not trashed my dearest treasures. *Chiron Rev* 12(1):11 Sp 93
If I have /risen up. *Purr* #3 75
If I have shown some of my emotions. *Guts* #6 89
If I have /trouble. *Wormwood Rev* 21(3):72 81
If I knew my suicide father in. *AAW*
If I listened, how persuaded might I get. *Bonesauce* #9:5 [89?]
If I made a cinnamon cake. *Latitudes* 2(3):43 Su/Fa 70
If I marinated my balls with alum. *Guts* #6 89
If I penned. *N; Po Eastwest* #2:6 68
If I put down. *Wisconsin Rev* 8(4):17 [75]
If I quarrel. *WWCD*
If I revive what was defunct. *Wormwood Rev* 31(4):130 91
If I said /I have a picture. *Wormwood Rev* 21(3):51 81
If I said /your cunt is like. *Wisconsin Rev* 10(4):32 Se 75

If I should embrace several extremes. *Fell Swoop* #28 [93?]
If I should ever be a seaman. *WWSL; Chrysalis* 8(7/8):12 55
If I should /peel out of. *TM; Red Clay Reader* #2 65
If I start telling you all of. *Reflektion* p20 My/Ju 90
If I strangled an ox. *Simbolica* #20:6 [61?]
If I thought /your breasts. *Baby John* #5:16 Nv 72
If I took. *Wormwood Rev* 20(4):130 80
If I turned out. *Mag* #5:51 73
If I was rigged. *Wind* 10(36):9 80
If I were as dedicated a poet as Lyn. *TH*
If I were ever worth damnation, it. *MAT*
If I were /God. *GMV; Studio One* p15 Sp 86
If I /were not. *Wormwood Rev* 21(3):84 81
If I would shoot Norman Mailer. *TDV; Stone Drum* 1(4):47 [86]
If I've been /yoked up. *Blank Gun Silencer* #4:24 Sp 92
If innocence. *Goliards* #7:96 Je 69
If it is an objective to strike out what. *CM*
If it is neat. *N; Cafe Solo* #4:15 Fa 72
If it is /what I am getting at. *Wormwood Rev* 21(3):50 81
If /it looks like. *Wormwood Rev* 24(1):10 84
If it were not my deliberate intention. *S*
If it were /not that difficult. *Wildflower* #2 De 81
If my ass. *Wormwood Rev* 21(3):58 81
If my bemusement at the futility of. *Innisfree Mag* 12(2):2 Fe 93
If my ears. *N; New Voices (New Paltz, NY)* #5:233 76
If my fragmented. *Wormwood Rev* 15(2):68 75
If my /youth. *Invisible City* #5:14 My 72
If Noah had built a flying machine. *S*
If one should be thought a freak because of. *Lactuca* #14:38 My 91
If only I /had two cocks. *Happiness Holding Tank* #10 73
If pussy /is not. *Thunder Sandwich* #4 85
If she had spoken, if I. *CM*
If she has a finger or two in her. *Shockbox* 1(5):13 92
If some Guru had waited for me. *Post Motel* #5 [92?]
If that beautiful body needs all. *Blind Horse Rev* #2:4 Ja/Fe 93
If that body of yours were more slender. *Wormwood Rev* 31(4):128 91
If the ambiance of the air about. *Guts* #6 89
If the bark comes off the sheen of branch. *Lactuca* #12:39 Fe 89

If the beginning were clear—a new land. *CM*
If the death of the hero is to carry. *Zerx Catalog* 3d ed:6 Oc 92
If the gods were weeping it is for. *MAT*
If the horror. *Madrona* 3(8):31 74
If the hurt has held us. *Flame* [1(1)] Sp 54
If the lady likes black leather, yet. *Wormwood Rev* 31(4):126 91
If the shoe fits. *IBG*
If the widow. *Grimoire* #4:19 Sp 83
If this is my motion. *Tawté* p21 My 75
If those bodies are only objects—. *Lactuca* #14:37 My 91
If those memories have left me, how. *Wormwood Rev* 24(1):10 84
If walking were a means of getting some-. *MAT*
If we are gentle in the frosty air, who. *Kindred Spirit* #15:15 Sp 88
If we set out to find an ocean, we found. *Tarasque* #2 84 85
If you dare publish these love poems, was. *MAT*
If you ever heard that Bulltoven pasted. *MAT*
If you freaked. *Wormwood Rev* 21(3):83 81
If you had /fallen. *Scree* #6 76
If you have ever seen dragon-flies fuck-. *Shockbox* 1(7/8):18 93
If you insist a nude photograph. *Guts* #6 89
If you think it is for me to put things. *Lucky Star* 2(5):8 Oc 86
If you were /a mountain. *Scree* #1 74
If you /were standing. *S; Wine Rings* 1(5):3 76
If you would be naked in the. *Wormwood Rev* 31(4):126 91
If your cunt /did not exist. *NC; TDV; Purr* #4 76
Imagination's, The. *Erratica.* 1(4):30 73
In 1935. *Wormwood Rev* 21(3):58 81
In a 350-thousand-word memoir of Henry. *Wormwood Rev* 27(4):92 87
In a bar. *Wormwood Rev* 15(4):156 75
In a big Stuben glass salver which. *TH*
In a moment of inspiration forty years ago. *AAW*
In an alcove. *SK*
In artifact. *PB; Epoch* 1(3):84 Sp 48
In brine relivened. *UWNB; Descant* 5(2) Win 61
In carnal trude among. *AP*
In fact. *SCA; Second Coming* 11(1/2):33 83
In less dreamy realm. *NN; Simbolica* #2 [51?]
In London city. *UWNB*

In my life. *Wormwood Rev* 5(3):16 65
In New York, according to E.B. White's. *GMV; Wind* 16(57):7 86
In presence of laughter. *HNH; N; P; PB; Sibylline* 1(2):116 Ap/Je 48
In reed of wound. *Wordjock* #4 Nv 68
In search of. *Cresset* 23(2):14 De 59
In spite of knowing better—and with. *MAT*
In Texas we got persimmons. *CM; Atom Mind* 3(11):62 Su 93
In the figure of a speech. *YMAN; Inferno* #2:9 [51?]
In the garden [T.D.]. *Deer and Dachshund* 1(1) Sp 51
In the Mobile Advanced Surgical Hospital. *TH*
In the name [T.D.]. *Miscellaneous Man* #3:14-16 Wi 54
In the rubble. *NC*
In this /hotel with. *Wormwood Rev* 21(3):80 81
In time of change. *Whetstone (Philad.)* 1(1):7 Sp 55
Indian girl preparing [C.F.]. *Free Lance* 2(2):10 54
Indifferences that I have ultimately, The *Fell Swoop* #28 [93?]
Indispensable nothingness that, The. *Shockbox* 1(7/8):26 93
Infernal engine that keeps chugging, The. *Asylum* 2(3):9 [?]
Initial description. *CYAM; HNH; HO; THYM; In/sert* 1(3) 57/58
Insistence on climate, An. *N; P; UWNB; Prairie Schooner* 32(3):193 Se 58
Instructions before Bartholomew. *Nimrod* 1(3):25 Sp 57
Interlude, An. *Wormwood Rev* 5(3):19 65
Intriguing thought---wouldn't you think, An. *BDS*
Inundated in slime, it was not even. *Shockbox* #4:30 92
Is a caress. *N*
Is it a question of having fallen---fallen. *TH*
Is it being caught up again in all. *Wormwood Rev* 31(4):127 91
Is it Really the verse-forms that im-. *Third Lung Rev* #6:5 90
Is it relinquishment when we give back. *TH*
Is it the moon's nadir that moves me. *S*
Is it tombs of wanting that hold me. *BDS; Open 24 Hours* #7 91
Is that /what. *Wormwood Rev* 21(3):54 81
Is the mouth. *BDS; Guts* #6 89
Is there a hiss of love as snakes get together. *NYQ* #41:68 Sp 90
Is there an end to it, an object---The brutal. *Bonesauce* #9:5 [89?]
Is this /her butt. *Zahir* 1(4/5):49 72
Is to be adult to be adulerous? *Ash* #7:28 Sp 91

It all. *Centering* #1 [73?]
It has not /departed. *NC*
It is a bravery to posit the inanimate. *Blind Horse Rev* #3:24 Ag/Se 93
It is almost as if there were never. *Wormwood Rev* 24(1):9 84
It is good, pulling the. *BDS; GMV; TDV; Puerto del Sol* 21(1):115 Su 85
It is not as if I am a salt-shaker. *MAT*
It is not /as if I /did not /know. *Tawté* p21 My 75
It is not /as if I imagined. *Wormwood Rev* 22(4):146 82
It is not as if I was getting. *Puerto del Sol* v18:134 Sp 83
It is not /dreaming. *N*
It is not Golgotha—it is. *CM; Pembroke Mag* #15:106 83
It is not the idea of any returning, it is. *Truly Fine* p8 Sp 90
It is only eternity. *Illuminations* #3:20 Su 67
It is snowing. *Thirteen* 5(3):34. Ap 87
It is the children who are condemned. *GMV; Pembroke Mag* #19 87
It is the nature of things that I am. *Gypsy* #14 90
It looks /like. *Blackberry* #9:34 At 78
It seems the besetting curse of generic man's. *Chiron Rev* 11(1):2 Sp 92
It was assumed a God-head. *CM*
It was her mood to undress her-. *Guts* #6 89
It was many sad, naked. *HO; Old Hickory Rev* 15(1):17 Sp/Su 83
It was /not. *Wormwood Rev* 15(2):67 75
It was /not a question. *Cafe Review* 3(7/8):18 Jl/Ag 92
It was not as if I was getting. *TDV; Puerto del Sol* v18:134 Sp 83
It was not blue wine I was. *Dog River Rev* 6(1):47 Sp 87
It was not that Bulltoven was going deaf. *Wormwood Rev* 26(3):86 86
It was not the high eminence, the. *Paper Bag* 2(2):28 Sp 90
It was not /wanted. *Thirteen* 5(4):4 Jl 87
It was only her very high standards—talking. *Tandava* v14:14 My 88
It was some sort of thought in my. *Black Gun Silencer* #3:10 Wi 91/92
It wasn't /a burglar alarm. *Wormwood Rev* 21(3):66 81
It wasn't as if the door opened. It was. *Third Lung Press* #4:4 89
It wasn't /her cunt. *Purr* #5 76
It wasn't /like floating. *Purr* #3 75
It's a hard /spurt. *Truly Fine* p8 Sp 90
It's a kind of plague that diseases my mind. *Wormwood Rev* 25(3) 85
It's a magnetic, kinetic buzz or vibe. *Bouillabaisse* #2:12 92
It's an indulgence, it's a sin, it's a vice—I love. *Gypsy* #12/13:55 89

It's been /there. *Wormwood Rev* 21(3):79 81
It's enough to give the literary world. *AAW*
It's never /so simple. *Wormwood Rev* 21(3):55 81
It's not that she led me on. *CM*
It's not /the body. *Wormwood Rev* 21(3):76 81
It's the job of turning the head back around. *Lucky Star* 2(1):11 Oc 84
It's the Sly-Wolf-Fart, that huge. *CM*
It's waking. You awoke me. It's bright. *CM*
Jack on a day at Olympus. *AP; SC; Three Hands* #4 52
Jaime Stong's aunt's tits. *TDV; Another Chicago Mag* #9 83
Japanese garden. *Wormwood Rev* 4(1):25 64
"Jerome," as in the sacrosanct Sup-. *Bouillabaisse* #2:12 92
Jesus hombre. *Illuminations* #3:5 Su 67
Jesus Ranch. *Wormwood Rev* 15(2):69 75
Joint between the cannon bone and pastern, The. *Earwig* #3 Oc 90
Jonquil, star-clustered. *Bleb* #6 Nv 72
Judas: a funeral lilt. *Black Cat Rev* #3 Je 65
Jujube. *Crescendo* 1(2) Nv 41
Jungle [C.F.]. *DB; TM*
Junior. *Westminster* 35(4):7. Wi 46/47
Karen's face was instantly brighter when. *Eotu* De 90
Key, The. *NC*
Key that no lock will fit, A. *Post Motel* #6 [92?]
Kicks. *Po Eastwest* #6:36 73
Kid /around so. *Lucky Star* 1(3):37. Ap 83
Kid Kokay Kokay. *AFTT; Ante* 1(2):21 Fa 64
Kind, no winsome maid would question. *Theo* 1(1) [Sp 64?]
Kind of houseboat of the mind, A. *AAW*
Kind of knowledge empty as dreaming, A. *CM*
Kine level the mane desire. *WWSL; Po* 76(3):134-5 Je 50
King Haul to Rome. *Wordjock* #4 Nv 68
King Kang. *Greenfield Rev* #3:49 52
King's lost Astor, The. *YMAN*
Kingdom's utter rail, A. *HNH; PB; Po* 75(3):145 De 49
Kissing. *N*
Kitchen-midden. *LYS*
Kneeling. *Scree* #13/14 79
Knight who lost his calling and left, The. *Shockbox* 1(6):19 [93?]

Knocking. *Reflektion* p20 My/Ju 90
Knowing. *Pot-hooks and Hangers* 1(2):11 Sp 74
Kumrad kumrad. *MHC*
Kunst Lear peel so white. *AP; OWH; Epos* 6(1):18 Fa 54
Kurt the in caper. *FSAB; OWH; Galley Sail Rev* #2:17 Sp 59
Kyle Merkle lead tard bassal. *MLM*
Ladies mags, The [T.D.]. *Sum* #7 Ap 65
Lady whose certainty is, A. *Thunder Sandwich* #3 85
Lament, lament. *RFA*
Lamenting the demijohn's passing. *Puerto del Sol* 12(2):45 Mr 73
Landscape with bather. *Star-web Paper* #8:9 84
Landscape with sunlight and death. *Bozart-Westminster* At 42
Language of keening, The. *UWNB; Descant* 5(2) Wi 61
Large, long, white radishes—if such. *MAT*
Large muscular, A. *Montana Gothic* #3:17 At 75
Larval calibration, The. *AP; Deer and Dachshund* #4 [53?]
Lash, The. *Wormwood Rev* 3(2):18 63
Last sacrament [C.F.]. *Olivant* Q [#2]:60 4th ¼ 53
Last /September's ox. *Scree* #13/14 79
Late Paul Zweig has been credited—or. *Wormwood Rev* 31(4):129 91
Laughing in a window—the half-image. *TH*
Laughing my ass off—would that con-. *Wormwood Rev* 31(4):124 91
Lay mystigog. *IBG; Olivant* Q #1(9) Se 53
Lead away—is that it: that we are lead. *MAT*
Leaf high in the gain. *Forum* 9(2):16 Su 71
League of lies, A. *NN*
Leaning her elbow. *Wildflower* #37 Je 4 86
Leaping /quagmires. *Thirteen* 5(4):4 Jl 87
Lease of ruin, The. *Penumbra* #11 Fa 72
Leave it in. *Hearse* #6:19 59
Led away—is that it: that we are led *See:* Lead away.... *MAT*
Leg of reason, A. *Goliards* #2 64
Legacy of war, The. *Quixote* 5(4):28 69
Legend of Lear, The. *TH*
Lemon Mayoley. *Showcase* #3:28 Jl 66
Leopard sleek as night, A. *Hearse* #7:12 [60]
Less. *Corduroy* #4:7 72
Less sinister. *CCM*

Lesson from the masters, A. *AFTT; Coffin* #1 [65?]
Lest flesh be burned. *Free Lance* 8(1):6 64
Let the Odong tree [T.D.]. *Deer and Dachshund* 1:1 Sp 51
Let the stone cry its mercy is lost. *YMAN*
Let us figure it out sometime in the calm. *Amelia* 3(2):91 Sp 86
Let's get. *Wormwood Rev* 15(2):64 75
Letter for home. *Blue Grass* #2:24 Wi 63
Letter to Bill. *Wormwood Rev* 5(3):22 65
Letter to Scott Greer. *N; YMAN; Po Fund J* 1(3) Fa 60
Lettuce formula. *Elizabeth* #5:9 Mr 63
Lettuce heart, A. *N; White Arms* [#1] Ap 74
Levitation may be linked to magic. *Flame* 5(1):6 Sp 58
Lie of dreams, The [C.F.]. *Miscellaneous Man* #2:19 Su 54
Lies for a sick child. *IH*
Life class. *UWNB*
Life /in my book. *Star-web Paper* #6:31 77
Light beer, A. *S*
Light of the sundered will, The. *Flame* 3(4):9 Wi 56
Light years. *Crop Dust* #2/3:35 Au/Wi 80
Like medieval female holy anorexics. *Impetus* Male#2:29 Ag 90
Limits of reality, The. *UWNB; Descant* 4(3) Sp 60
Lines written in a city jail. *P; PLS*
Lips, The. *TDV; Look Quick* #11 Fa 83
Listless against granite. *YDHT*
Little home scene. *HPH; N; Evergreen Rev* #28:35 Ja/Fe 63
Little shitter. *Wormwood Rev* 21(3):78 81
Little strange knoll. *HNH; Blue Guitar* #13:10 Fa 57
Loath rake in velvet safari. *IBG; Illiterati* #6 55
Loaf of, A. *Wormwood Rev* 21(3):62 81
Lob lag Sweezey Street. *AP*
Lobotomy. *Wormwood Rev* 3(2):17 63
Long line, A. *BDS; HSA; Zahir* 2(2):52 76
Look at that stripéd dog pissing on. *Pig in a Pamphlet* #10 85
Losing. *MS*
Losing you. *Wind* #9:16 73
Loss in holy gain. *Po Fund J* 1(2) Su 60
Lost harvest, The. [T.D.] *Po Book Mag* 7(2):5 Wi 55
Lot of bull, A. [C.F.] *SScribe* p49 [57?]

Lotus bud. [W.E.B.] *Naked Ear* #6 [58?]
Love poem /(for Mildred). *UTEV; Psychology Today* 3(2) Jl 69
Love without coverage. *Blue Beat* p6 Mr 64
Lovers, The. *N; TWBS; Po* 85(6):337 Mr 55
Luckless brethren. *Free Lance* 6(1):18 60
Lucy Bulltoven slime. *AP; Deer and Dachshund* #4 [53?]
Lucy Bulltoven with. *New: American & Canadian Po* #12:6 Ap 70
Lugubrious meanderer. *Kindred Spirit* 7(3):7 Wi 88/89
Luminous invisible stone, The. *YMAN; Whetstone (Philad.)* 2(2):78 57
Lyric for this hour—for this day. *Span* 1(1) Ap/My 41
Lyric /I know a girl. *Beat of Wings* p11 Jl 41
Mac Bulltoven Clyde. *AP; YMAN; Deer and Dachshund* #4 [53?]
Macaroni heap of, A. *TH*
Mad dog. *GMV; Wormwood Rev* 20(4):129 80
Maiden whalen. *Arx* 2(1):34 My 68
Making it. *South Florida Po J* 1(3):76 Sp 69
Making or unmaking of what, The. *AAW*
Malcolm X. *S*
Male and female. [T.D.] *Sheaf* #1:14 Ja 55
Mallory's. *Premiere* #7:8 69
Mama's boy. *Song* #3/4:45 [77?]
Mammoth of earth. *Aldebaran Rev* #2:15 68
Man against numbers. *Chrysalis* 6(5/6):13 53
Man against time. *Charas* 2(3)/#4 72
Man and God. *Wanderlust* 1(2):27 Jl 58
Man and race. [T.D.] *Free Lance* 2(2):24 54
Man-child. *Desert Rev Penny Poetry Sheet* #2 63
Mangled, A. *Wormwood Rev* 15(2):62 75
Mannequin-like certainty, A. *Bonesauce* #6 89
Many islands. *IBG; Zebra* #10:35 Nv 54
Margaret's shameless career. *YMAN; Struggle* 1(1) Fe 54
Margie II comes flip-flopping down the stairs. She has. *MAT*
Marina with orange. *Coercion Rev* #2:13 Sp 59
Marine. *Earthjoy* #2 72
Marriage of love, The. *OWH; Intro* 1(3/4):149 51
Marsh gut. *Aldebaran Rev* #2:17 68
Martyred. *Another Chicago Mag* #5 80
Mary, Mary. *Suck-egg Mule* #3/4 [52?]

Mastered. *White Arms* [#1] Ap 74
Masturbating. *N*
Matador. *S*
Matadora. *N; TWBS; Po* 85(6):337 Mr 55
Mate baiting. *Jeopardy* 8:139 72
Mating, The. [T.D.] *Struggle* 1(3) Ap 54
May fall. *N; NN; NM q Rev* 16(3):352 At 46
Maybe /after. *SP*
Maybe it is /my funeral. *NC*
Meathodical sea nymphe, The. *See:* Methodical sea nymphe, The
Medical science. *SP*
Medley. *PLS; American Writing* p83 42
Mel por adore. *Mississippi Rev* 1(2):36 72
Meld, or eclat of your pillow-talk, The. *NYQ* #45:51 91
Melodia you will not find. *HO; Old Hickory Rev* 15(1):18 Sp/Su 83
Melon bosomed. *SK*
Memento for man—Heine. *Whetstone (Philad.)* 4(2):60 61
Memoirs of a ripening quince. *Curled Wire Chr* 2(3):9 Nv 54
Memorandum /There are. *OWH; Epos* 7(4):19 Su 56
Memorial. [T.D.] *Naked Ear* #6 [58?]
Memorial of love. *MLM*
Memory. *Pig Iron* #8:43 80
Memory is a broken knife. *See:* Poem /Memory is a broken knife
Memory, memory. *N; Goodly Co.* #15 Ap 70
Men and women that. *FSAB; N; Sparrow (W. Lafayette)* #11 Ap 59
Metamorphoses of the third wheel. *N; OWH; Inferno* #3:14 [51?]
Metaphor hempen long, The. *Simbolica* #11 [54]
Metaphysics, A. *NC*
Metaphysics, also astronomy. [C.F.] *Suck-egg Mule* #1 [51?]
Methodical sea nymphe, The. *Wordjock* #4 Nv 68
Mickey-the-Mack built a rustic shack. *MAT; Ash* #8:14 Su 91
Mill girl Saturday night. *Poet & Critic* File#2:19 Ap 62
Millenium. *Blitz* [#2?] [64?]
Milto set. *MOS*
Mime. *Green Horse for Po* 1(2):36 73
Missing most. *Northeast* p34 Sp/Su:70
Mistaken identity, The. *Folio* 2(2):42 Fa 66
Moat sin lal. *GMV; OWH; TDV; Black Mountain Rev* #7:189 Ag 57

Mock suicide. [C.F.] *Miscellaneous Man* #4:23 Sp 55
Monstrance, A. *Simbolica* #6 [52?]
Monstrous, A. *Bonesauce* #11:5 [89?]
Montage of all varied things—I have, The. *Rag Mag* 11(1):41 93
Moon sprung. [T.D.] *Neo* p6 Sp/Su 54
Moon's shroud is a weepy, The. *BDS; Kindred Spirit* 7(3):7 Wi 88/89
Moonth of jaunt, The. *AFTT; Ante* 1(2):20 Fa 64
Moot theme. *NN; Iconograph* #3 Fa 46
Morality, A. *IBG; Westminster* 37(1):14 Sp 48
More /I think, The (1). *Wormwood Rev* 22(4):146 82
More /I think, The (2). *Wormwood Rev* 24(2):73 84
More tart, A. *Star-web Paper* #6:32 77
Morgue: a study in dementia, The. *Bozart-Westminster* Wi 39/40
Morning after, The. [C.F.] *Struggle* 1:1 Fe 54
Mortal cone in middle brawn. *Jacaranda* #6:7 Fe 66
Mortal level. *NN*
Mortification of flesh. *See:* Psalm for the mortified flesh
Morton gleaning pebbles. *AP; Sheaf* #1:7 Ja 55
Most /goddamned, The. *Wormwood Rev* 21(3):64 81
Most of our rhymsters. *Margarine Maypole* #64 Ag 84
"Mother, oh my mother," the monster. *Dog River Rev* 8(2):24 At 89
Motion of greening, The. *HNH; In/sert* 1(3) 57/58
Mountain as. *River* p15 Sp 60
Mountain penial, The. *Wormwood Rev* #3 61
Mountain winter. *DRA; YMAN*
Mud-hut. *Simbolica* #27:31 [62]
Mulhaven. *N; Loco Motives* [#1?] 72
Multiple end, The. *SCV; WWSL; Three Hands* #4 52
Multiple hosts, The. *OWH; Humanist* 10(6):247 50
Multiple rooms of the heart sealed, The. *Minotaur* #24(13) 91
Multitudinous surrender, A. *Galley Sail Rev* #14:24 64
Muse over. *Intrepid* #7 Mr 67
Mussgrave. *Elizabeth* #13:26 Jl 69
Mute tambourine. *NN*
Mute wonder your. [C.F.] *Neo* p17 Sp/Su 54
My breathing. *N; Wine Rings* 1(5):2 76
My chiefest grief is that I have no grief—. *Ash* #8:14 Su 91
My cock. *Wormwood Rev* 21(3):72 81

My flesh was never weak, nor my spirit. *AAW*
My girls. *Wormwood Rev* 21(3):60 81
My infirmity. *FSAB*
My lady. *SP*
My /libidinal. *Fell Swoop* #26/27 [92?]
My measurement. *Simbolica* #24:18 [62?]
My mode. *NC*
My new revelation for the day. *AFTT; N*
My old typewriter is dead. It is. *Chiron Rev* 11(1):2 Sp 92
My penis is a. *Shockbox* 1(6):33 [93?]
My reproaches. *MLM*
My saddest commentary on the human. *Writers Forum* 14 88
My studio, as I call it—where I *Chiron Rev* 11(1):2 Sp 92
My turn. *Foxfire* 2(2):29 Je 68
My waning bravery. [C.F.] *Deer and Dachshund* 1(3) [53?]
Mystery, The. *Wormwood Rev* 21:3 81
Mystical borders, The. *Mummy* #2:15 63/64
Myths of. *Attention Please* 1(2):21 76
Nacreous shell of the large, The. *BDS; Pembroke Mag* #17:204 85
Naked boys. *New: American & Canadian Po* #12:7 Ap 70
Naked tombs. *HPH; Elizabeth* #5:10 Mr 63
Nakedly, the limp rain. [T.D.] *Po Book Mag* 7(2):6 Wi 55
Nakedness of, The. [C.F.] *SScribe* p51 [57?]
Naming of trees, The. *Wormwood Rev* 7(3/4):35 67
Narration as mobile. *YMAN; Simbolica* #7 [53?]
Narwhal buck roe. *MHC*
Nations and people living on the edge of a death wish. *NP*
Native apostrophe. *WYTC*
Navel, A. *Star-web paper* #6, 32 77
Nestor's white plague. *IBG; Bridge* 7(3):80 Mr 53
Never having noticed. *Wisconsin Rev* 8(4):16 [75]
Nevidation cumlaud. *Madrona* 3(8):30 74
Next to the last remedy. *Westminster* 44(4):14 Wi 54/55
Night. *N; NDCN; P; TWBS; Kansas Mag* p43 57
Night is, The. *NC*
Nimbus of. *Gypsy* #14 90
No cuckold so gleeful. *AFTT; Ante* 1(1):17 64
No dog. *Wormwood Rev* 21(3):64 81

No father where the. *CCM; IBG; Rough Weather* #1:8 Fa50/Sp 51
No female. *Small Pond* #18:12 Wi 70
No hepty tall, moon, moon. *AP; Deer and Dachshund* #4 [53?]
No, I don't. *Simbolica* #31:14 [63?]
No, I mean it. *SK*
No, I /never. *Wormwood Rev* 15(2):66 75
No load yet laid down. *MHC*
No sane rigor leafing through. *MHC*
No sinister wreath. *AFTT; Southwest Rev* v49:330 At 64
No special whistle. *CCM; P; Rough Weather* #1:7 Fa 50/Sp 51
No stopping it. *Aldebaran Rev* #8 [70?]
No ultimate sacrilege. *Sumac* 1(2):67 Wi 69
No weal like mighty Adam gave. *YMAN; Archer* 4(2):[3] Su 54
Noble bull. *Po Dial* 1(2):34 Sp 61
Nobody /can say. *Wormwood Rev* 21(3):67 81
Noir is the niche, their ratty hair. *Shockbox* 1(5):13 92
Noose, The. *AFTT; N; Po Now* #36:38 82
Not all cunt is the same—surpris-. *Guts* #6 89
Not having. *GMV; TDV; Southwestern American Lit* 8(2):34 Sp 83
Not letting a feeling bud out. *Wormwood Rev* 31(4):124 91
Not that I had ever needed a horse's. *Wormwood Rev* 27(4):91 87
Not unfriendly exchange, A. *Wisconsin Rev* 10(4):31 Se 75
Note in passing. [C.F.] *DB; TM; Free Lance* 3(1):9 55
Note on timorous day, A. *Blue Guitar* 1:3 De 52
Now beholden. *Intrepid* #6 66
Now for a quicky, Mr. Dickey—a. *Conditioned Response* #8:4 [88?]
Now that murder is fluid. *OWH; Simbolica* #11 54
Now your breasts. *Santa Fe po* #2:11 Sp 82
Nude, against light, A. *N; TWBS; Miscellaneous Man* #10:11 Ja 57
Nude hula-hoop contest was to be, The. *Thunder Sandwich* #4 85
Nude /with small breasts, A. *Stone* 3(1/2):9 Wi/Su 70
Number many number man. *Quartet* 3(18):10 Sp 67
Number season. [C.F.] *In/sert* 1(4) 62
Nuptials [C.F.] *Naked Ear* #1 [Wi 56]
O desperation we claim as our. *Cafe Review* 3(7/8):18 Jl/Ag 92
O if the brilliance of the sunset were all. *GMV*
O mighty. *Black Sun* 1(5):19 66
Oasis. [C.F.] *DB; TM*

Obedience, The. *NC*
Oberseen hurst leading. *Harlequin* 1(1):4 Sp 64
Objectification of perception, An. *Simbolica* #9 53
Objective love. [T.D.] *Signet* 3(9):11 Oc 61
Objects. *NC; Po Now* #26:22 80
Oblique. *Scree* #3 75
Oboe amble. *COM; Bridge* 4(8):223 My 50
Ocean, The. *NC*
Ode for one who did not die. *Crescendo* 1:3 Ja 42
Of a disposed lover. [C.F.] *Simbolica* #15 [58?]
Of cosmic sanction. *FSAB; OWH*
Of credible beatitudes. *CYAM; HO; THYM; UWNB; Fresco* ns#1:62 Fa
   60
Of deathless law. *HPH; P; Genesis West* #1:236 Sp 63
Of dextrous civility. *Pegasus* 4(3)/#15 56
Of fatal anguish. [T.D.] *Olivant* Q [#2]:44 4th ¼ 53
Of rubies and cherries. *Bridge* 4(6):182 Mr 50
Of self bequeath. *Illuminations* #6 Su 72
Of the feather floating there. *Existaria* #7:16 Se/Oc 57
Of the self exceeded. *HNH*
Of ultimate knowledge. *YMAN; Nimrod* 3(3):34 Sp 59
Oh beach love blossom. *UTEV*
Oh, beautiful. *SK*
Oh Phoenicians. *UWNB; Epos* 5(3):24 Sp 54
Oh precious the unkneaded dough. *Miscellaneous Man* #1:19 Ap 54
Oh that /atomic blasted. *Harlequin* 3(2):13 Fa 66
Oh, the marine langour. *AP; Deer and Dachshund* #4 [53?]
Oh, the weathered. *SK*
Oh, wonder city that. [T.D.] *Literary Calendar* p9 Su 56
Old and secret. *WWSL; Cresset* 19(8):40 Je 56
Old car left where the, An. *GMV; TDV; Pig in a Pamphlet* #10 85
Old /court yard, The. *Bonesauce* #9(14) [89]
Old crab with a cracked shell, the Zodiac. *Thunder Sandwich* #3 85
Old crone, An. *N; Simbolica* #27:31 [65?]
Old stallion has his black cock, The. *Wormwood Rev* 26(3):85 86
On a bale. *Maelstrom Rev* 6(1/2):49 81
On a theme from a surrealist. *WWSL; Chicago Rev* 5(1):19 Wi 50
On artifact. *See:* In artifact

On contemplating certain loss. *NN; Voices* #130:23 Su 47
On the essence of faith. *TWBS*
On the floor. *Wormwood Rev* 21(3):63 81
Once and for all. *Grande Ronde Rev* 2(1):21 67
Once, telling about the delight of Unt-. *TH*
One fondles /his cock. *SK*
One stroke of a samurai's sword. *Bitterroot* #92:39 Wi 87/88
One, teen-like. *SK*
One thing and another, she said, being. *Thunder Sandwich* #4 85
One X. *N*
Only death is discipline. *Upsurge* #10:6 [50?]
Only transubstantiation of host I know, The. *AAW*
Open. *Wormwood Rev* 15(2):66 75
Open up, Crews, this is a citizen's. *Art Mag* #5 86
Or even human hands. *Potpourri* 1(2) Su 64
Order in my life, or my life-time, The. *Open 24 Hours* #6(14) 89
Order of law, The. *HNH; P; V*
Otherwise /gull sentineled. *Stone Country* 74(2):17 My 74
"Our lives teach us who we are"—. *MAT; Chiron Rev* 12(1):11 Sp 93
Our pertinence. *Wind* #9:15 73
Our two faces juxtaposed. *Post Motel* #7 [92?]
Our weather of love. [T.D.] *Free Lance* 2(2):23 54
Out of. *Washington Rev* 5(5) Fb/Mr 80
Out yonder. *PLS*
Outside that I have turned in, The. *Descant* 30(1):30 F/W 85/86
Over life-size. *Free Lance* 2(1):28 54
Over the kill and through the blood. *MHC; NDC*
Ox is stolid, The. *BDS; Rio Grande Writers Assn Chbk* #5:11 Fa 89
P. *A*
Pagan. *Unmuzzled Ox* 1(4) At 72
Page itself was part of the meaning, The. *Flame* 1(4):1 Wi 54
Pale Saltimbanque, The. *N*
Palimpsest. *YMAN; Whetstone (Philad.)* 4(2):61 61
Pan-verde terra. *Centering* #2 [73?]
Pants awkward. *TDV; Another Chicago Mag* #9 83
Pap oh honey dandy. *Olivant q* #1:9 Se 53
Paraclete. [T.D.] *Naked Ear* #8 [58?]
Parade of one person, A. *GMV; Crescent Rev* 5(1):63 87

Pierre, submerged and floating. *Camels Coming* #1 Ag 65
Pilum melongena nudiped. *AP; OWH; Experiment* 6(4) 53
Pink chamber's privacy, The. *WWSL; Free Lance* 2(1):27 54
Pisces is. *S*
Pizzicato. [T.D.] *Deer and Dachshund* 1(1) Sp 51
Place, The. *Wormwood Rev* 20(4):126 80
Plain sun, The. *Wormwood Rev* 15(2):60 75
Plant this seed oh goddess of. *WWSL; Montevallo Rev* 1(3):54 Sp 52
Pleasant enough evening, A. *Conditioned Response* #7:23 [87?]
Plum child. *GMV; OWH; Black Mountain Rev* #7:187 Ag 57
Plum tree, The. *Signet* 3(6):9 Je 61
Poem /Can't quite be, A. *NC*
Poem—Cock of crowing. *Whispers* Fe 41
Poem—I'm tiring of this broken land. *Whispers* Mr 41
Poem /Memory is a broken knife. *Westminster* 40(2):12 Sp 51
Poem /She claimed. *Aim* 1(2):30 70
Poem /Your breasts are the sea surge. *Raven Anth* #76:10 Ap 48
Poem to love. *Arx* #10:49 Fe 68
Poem: Un-. *PLS*
Poems /I'll keep. *Wormwood Rev* 21(3):[88] 81
Poet facing up to life, The. *AFTT; N; Po* 105(5):308 Fe 65
Poet's breath, A. *SP; Intrepid* #7 Mr 67
Poet's premier need is to supersede, The. *GMV.*
Poise of restless wonder, The. *NDCN; PB; TWBS; Po* 75(3):148 De 49
Poisoned springs of my unction, The. *Chiron Rev* 11(1):2 Sp 92
Politics they. *Loco Motives* [#1?] 72
Polyglot in sublime. *WWSL; Cresset* 19(1):70 Nv 55
Port wound bracing loss. *UWNB; Sparrow (W. Lafayette)* #16:10 De 61
Port's eye, the blooming wind thick as melanin. *MHC*
Portugal, Portugal, sea. *UWNB; Blue Guitar* #20 Fa 62
Postmortem. *Penumbra* #10:21 Fa 71
Potaphor in a wretched wind. *N; OWH; Yugen* #1:7 58
Power engine, The. *Showcase* #2:9 Nv/De 65
Prayer for a deeper winter. *Flame* 1(1):0 Sp 54
Precept. *Galley Sail Rev* #14:24 64
Prescience. *Riverrun* 1(4) 67
Present, The. *Wormwood Rev* 21(3):63 81
Pride and hesitation. [C.F.] *DB; TM*

Prisoned at the edge of Pisa in. *Mallife* #22:37 Su 92
Procession, A. *BDS; Abraxas* #25/26:46 82
Profile for the loving critic. *Trace* #55:331-2 65
Projection past the beating lintel. *YMAN*
Proof for anabasis. *CCM; Simbolica* #1 [51?]
Prophet I turned out to be, The. *AFTT; Free Lance* 9(1):47 65
Proposition, The. *Nausea* 9:40 Fa 75
Prosody to carry you or jumping off, A. *Gulf Coast* 5(1):76 Su 92
Prospero in our midst. *MHC*
Protuberances like tadpoles—if they. *Graffiti Off the Asylum Walls*
    #1:17 Nv 92
Proverb, The. *Mati* #4:58 Wi/Sp 77
Psalm for a late season as the sea. *N; PLS; Iconograph* #2:[41] Mr 41
Psalm for the mortified flesh. *PLS; Phoenix* 2(1):91 Sp 39
Psalm for the sifting sands. *PLS*
Psalm of consolation. *P; PLS; WWA*
Psalm on a long way come. *PLS; S*
Psalms out of New Orleans. *See:* Poem: Un-; With its own hands
Pseudo pleuronectes americanus. *FSAB; HO; Hearse* [#1]:11 [57?]
Psuedo pleuronectes. *See:* Pseudo pleuronectes americanus
Pungent, boiling. *N; NC*
Purity. *Wild Dog* #11:14 Oc 64
Purity of an existence which was, The. *My Legacy* #11C:14 93
Purpose. *Green Horse for Po* 1(2):36 73
Pursy bartered. *Above Ground Rev* 3(2):47 Su 73
Put it down low. *Galley Sail Rev* #12:17 63
Put tea upon the spirit lamp. *YMAN; Nimrod* 6(2):7 [6-?]
Python's bold egg, The. *CCM; Bridge* 2(5) [48?]
Quality not of ether, A. *N; NN*
Queen sooth. *El Coqui* #1:46 Ca 77/78
Question now, The. *N; Stone Drum* 1(3):18 74
Question was never where would I be-, The. *Guts* #6 89
Quiet catastrophe come, The. *FSAB; Intro* 1(3/4):149 51
Quite suddenly. *Coffin* #1 [65?]
Race won in the hypertrophied loss. *MHC; YDP*
Rachel the wicked pie. *HPH; Signet* 3(9):4 Oc 61
Rage, The. *Stone Country* 75(2):11 My 75
Rain dogs. *AFTT*

Rain drenched. *Everyman* p74 Su 74
Rain from Heaven. *SK*
Rain in spring time. *AFTT; Elizabeth* #8:11 Mr 65
Rallied beyond censure. *IBG; Whetstone (Philad.)* 2(2):78 57
Rape. *Goliards* #7:59 Je 69
Rape, The. *IBG; N; Simbolica* #15 [58?]
Rattle roon hoady. *HPH; Experiment* 5(3) Fa 50
Raven leaf how share, The. *AP*
Rays cutting clouds like. *N*
Reaching. *Wormwood Rev* 15(2):64 75
Realm. *Baby John* #5:16 Nv 72
Reaper, The. *S*
Recapitulation. *NN; S*
Recently, I decided to go on the wagon. *BDS; Slipstream* #7:103 87
Recondite. [C.F.] *Sheaf* #3:17 Fe 56
Red cunning and creme de menthe. *Grist* 1(4) De 64
Red-mouthed. *NC; Po Now* #26:22 80
Redenigration. *CCM; Raven Anth* #72(10) Ap 47
Reductio ad absurdum. *Wormwood Rev* 5(2):31 65
Reel cadence the aphid. *SCV; WWSL; Three Hands* #4 52
Reeper, The. *See:* Reaper, The
Referential. *NN*
Regicide. *Head* #2 65
Rejoyce. *IBG; Gale* 1(11):1 De 49
Rel bore speng lule. *HPH; Outsider* #1:79 Fa 61
Relating a dream. *Back Door* 1(2):9 70
Remaining simpatico. *South Dakota Rev* 5(2):74 Su 67
Remembered to elder. *N*
Remorse is a useless passion. *Simbolica* #16:[7] 57
Remove toward po. *Goliards* #3:14 64
Renewable coupon, The. *Po Eastwest* #3(13) 70
Reno. [C.F.] *Naked Ear* #5 [57?]
Repairing to. *MO*
Reprehensible thunder. *El Coqui* #1:45 Ca 77/78
Requiem after murder. *Blue Grass* #2:23 Wi 63
Resemblances. *Po Now* 4(5):37 79
Residue or fall-out flaking my, The. *Writers Forum* #16:54 90
Resolve. [C.F.] *Quagga* 1(2):4 My 60

Restoration or restitution, The. *BDS; Dog River Rev* 8(2):24 At 89
Reth for wreath for ever. *Wild Dog* #8:23 My 64
Retreat [C.F.] *Naked Ear* #3 [57?]
Return not to returning. *NNH; Flame* 2(2):6 Su 55
Returned mariner, The. *Intrepid* #18/19:32 71
Returning to Taos, after many seasons. *CM; Pivot* #32:156 82
Revelation of senility, The. *FSAB; Nomad* #1:17 59
Revenge, The. *Black Sun* 1(5):19 66
Ridge reknown. *Centering* #2 [73?]
Right now I am not so very big. *Semina* #4 59
Rime upon the runic squalor. *Theo* 1(2) Fa 64
Ringed in a circle of singing so. *GMV; Writers Forum* 12 86
Rita was wearing a sequined bra, a low-. *GMV; Urbanus* p22 Su 88
River, The. *FSAB; N; Po* 91(4):259 Ja 58
River muted in thunder, The. *WWSL; Chrysalis* 8(7/8):11 55
River of mirth, The. *YMAN; Comprehension* 1(3):12 Wi 50/51
River of molten, The. *Simbolica* #1 [51?]
Riveted against time—is she dead. *Gypsy* #14 90
Roaring lion held dear, The. *MHC; Po Newsl (Albuq.)* #2 De 64
Robert said. *Wormwood Rev* 11(3):114 71
Rock wombed in the rhythm of night. *Encanto* 5:1 Ap/My 72
Rot, The. *Tequila Rev* #5:21 79
Round, The. *IBG; Naked Ear* #7 [58?]
Roundest of, The. *Lemming* #2:13 Wi 72
Rounding the horn. *AP; Sheaf* #2:14 Nv 55
Ruby left a strange impression. *Ash* #5:10 Fa 90
Ruin in our flesh, The. *HPH; Po* 95(5):293 Fe 60
Sacer Jane-cat dotal. *Goliards* #1 64
Sacristy. *Blue Grass* #2:25 Wi 63
Safe and sane remembrance. *Sheaf* #3:15 Fe 56
Saffron and honey. *SP*
Said ever the raisen crane. *TWBS; Departure* #8:11 [55?]
Sallow ring the left pervading. *MHC; YDP*
Sallow sallow the sign yet wreathed. *WWSL; Po* 76(3):132-3 Je 50
Salty azure in an old lighthouse tower. *Descant* 30(1):30 Fa/Wi 85/86
Salver of ruin, The. *Charas* 2(3)/#4 72
San Francisco. *Telephone* #10 75
Sand storm: Texas prairie. *Bozart-Westminster* Wi 37/38

Sand wind—sand sea. *Arx* 2(2):36 Jn 68
Sand, coarse as. *S*
Sand-blasting. *VRG; Wormwood Rev* 15(2):61 75
Sand-blotched, The. *E*
Sand storm: Texas prairie. *Bozart-Westminster* Wi 37/38
Sane grew leven Pete. *AP*
Sardis, where did I. [C.F.] *Deer and Dachshund* 1(2) [52?]
Sated in lucid divine. *AP; HNH; Sparrow (W. Lafayette)* #1:12 Ju 54
Satiety. *Goliards* #1 64
Scene who. *TWBS; Idiom* 1(2):96 Su 53
Scepter's cold dissonance, The. *Head* #2 65
Scream-, A. *S*
Sea piece. *Cyclotron* 3(1):10 Sp 65
Seal of approbation. *Mummy* #2:15 63/64
Search the mythical dawn. *Head* #2 65
Seascape. *Bridge* 4(9):281 Je 50
Season lost past favor, The. *AFTT; Dion* #5:6 65
Season of autumn light. *Sumac* 1(2):68 Wi 69
Season of rain, The. *PB*
Season of surrender, The. *Inland* 2(2):15 At 58
Season, season, tart so red. *AFTT*
Season sour last to hew. *UWNB; Blue Guitar* #16 Fa 59
Seasons, The. *Cottonwood Rev* p11 Fa 70
Seathed the sear recanter. *Spearhead* 2(2):22 Sp 51
Secret, The. *Whetstone (Huntsville, TX)* 2(1):16 Fa 68
Secret order, The. *TM; Per/se* 1(1):50 Sp 66
Section VII and all. *HPH; Kansas Mag* p32 59
Seeding season. *Greenfield Rev* 1(4):51 Sp 71
Seeing an /old girl. *Coldspring J* #8:16 Se 75
Seeing suddenly. *Wormwood Rev* 5(3):21 65
Seeker. *Wormwood Rev* 1(3) 61
Seeking to. *N*
Self refracted, the grim last mead. *Head* #2 65
Senile. *Wormwood Rev* 9(1):26 69
Sequence. *El Coqui* #2:32 Ta 78
Sequence of violence, The. *Harlequin (Sherman, TX)* 4(1):27 Sp 67
Serpent of God, The. [C.F.] *TM; DB*
Serving God-all-mighty. *YMAN*

Seven /years. *Wormwood Rev* 21(3):76 81
Seventh oracle. *NN; Raven Anth* #74:9 Oc 47
Several children. *N*
Several renowned poets of. *BDS; GMV; Pembroke Mag* #17:204 85
Severed scrotum, The. *MS*
Shadow, I might say. *Everyman* p74 Su 74
Shallow of lisping stones, The. *IBG*
Shameless. [C.F.] *DB; TM*
Shattered jewel, A. *HPH; P; Chicago Rev* 5(1):18 Wi 50
Shauna was determined not to. *Guts* #6 89
She came /from. *Scree* #3 75
She came out in black little Spanish. *CM*
She claimed. *See:* Poem /She claimed
She found her heights in. *CM; Tarasque* #2:83 85
She had /a lacquered hair style. *Desperado* #7 72
She had a lot of tinsel but her stems. *Pearl* #19:13 Fa/Wi 93
She had some schemes. Some were real. *AAW*
She hated rattlers. Does it matter. *CM; Po Now* #36:3 82
She knows that bed she'll go to. *AAW*
She laid a lot of eggs, blew them. *Pembroke Mag* #22:50 90
She loves me not. *DRA; YMAN*
She said she thought she saw me. *Crab Creek Rev* 7(2):28 Su 91
She said /you're. *GMV; Urbanus* p21 Su 88
She shut. *Grande Ronde Rev* #14.75 Sp 73
She was /a girl. *Wormwood Rev* 21(3):77 81
She was but a young girl hardly past. *GMV*
She was like a British sporting gentle-. *GDD*
She was showing me how to drink. Gypsy #21/22 Fa 93/Wi 94
She was /sure. *TH*
She was waiting. *Wormwood Rev* 9(1):26 69
She weary candle. *Look Quick* #4 Sp 76
Shit-, A. *Wormwood Rev* 21(3):52 81
Shore birds. *Stone* 3(1/2):12 Su 70
Shore divides me from the sea, The. *BDS; OMWF*
Shouldn't I have in some fever or fire. *Lucky Star* 2(5):8 Oc 86
Show me the knife. *UWNB; Cleveland Rev* 1(2) Wi/Sp 92
Shuck, A. *Wormwood Rev* 21(3):80 81
Shut the bud blooming in holy. *Yowl* #6:2 64

Si, si—Bermuda Espinosa was being ex-. *Tandava* v14:15 My 88
Sick with envy. If there had. *Impetus* #6:14 [85?]
Side, The. *MOS*
Sight as asinine mendicant. *HPH; Epos* 7(1):7 ^[Fa 55
Sigma for a zodiac. [C.F.] *DB; TM; Po Book Mag* 7(2):20 Wi 55
Signature, A. *Wormwood Rev* #80:130 80
Silenced curlew, The. *Whetstone (Huntsville, TX)* 3(2):27 Fa 69
Siler the fishyman's son. *AP*
Simply because of fear. *Gale* 1:10 Nv 49
Sin the seemly cannonade. *MHC; Jacaranda* #6:8 Fe 66
Since my design. *Wormwood Rev* 21(3):71 81
Sinecure they cried, A. *CYAM; FSAB; THYM; Inferno* #4:29 [51?]
Singer past the delectable light. *Head* #2 65
Single. *YCSW*
Sins, The. *Wormwood Rev* 15(2):63 75
Sketch, The. *Wind* 2(4):28 Wi/Sp 71/72
Skin diver. *YMAN*
Skin or sheen as it fails to coalesce. *Lactuca* #12:38 Fe 89
Slade Slatter in a down-draft drizzle. *Sum* #1:20 De 63
Slander that defiled the pale of wishes, The. *Aileron* 12:8 91
Sleep. *Purr* #4 76
Sleep disrupted by a nightmare, The. *Bonesauce* #11:8 [89?]
Sleep dweller. *CCM*
Sleep /swollen. *NC*
Sleep that joined us despite its terrors, The. *BDS*
Sleeping /a dream. *South Florida Po J* #4/5:187 70
Sleeping, your own needs possess you. *CM*
Slim long pool. *AP*
Sloe tree, bushed and spangled. *Out of Sight* 1(1):25 66
Slow cranes on bold wings. *PB*
Small anonymous men, The. *YMAN; Simbolica* #6 [53?]
Small /concrete. *Wormwood Rev* 21(3):81 81
Small irrigation, The. *Po Newsl (Philad.)* #19:4 [73?]
Small world. *Southwest Heritage* 9(2/3):31 Su/Fa 79
Smartly shod. *Blackbird Circle* #4:15 Sp 73
Smother heart I run. [C.F.] *SScribe* p50 [57?]
Smothered halo, The. *MHC*
Snake, The. *Wormwood Rev* 21(3):57 81

Snaked-out verbatim freak, The. *BDS; River Rat Rev* #4:17 88
Snare for the wind, A. *Nimrod* 4(2):7 Wi 60
Snowflakes that will not be, melting. *Tandava* Ja 91
So forlorn. [C.F.] *Suck-egg Mule* #1 [51?]
So her /breasts do not. *Wormwood Rev* 5(3):17 65
So I know. *Wormwood Rev* 15(2):59 75
So it happened you got a wood-tick. *CM*
So, Rexroth. *BDS; HSA; Hampden-Sydney Po Rev* Wi 76
So squalling. *Wormwood Rev* 15(2):65 75
So the dead did not die in vain? *Kapustkan* De 40
So they took. *MLM*
Soldier's memorial in dusk, A. *Arx* #11:36 Mr 68
Sole the fabled dim recess. *WWSL; Po* 88(1):18 Ap 56
Soliloquy at dusk. *NN*
Solo rail no rip is sung. *AP; Bridge* 11(6):94 Je 57
Solstice. *HF; Premiere* #7:7 69
Some aching. *Centering* #2 [73?]
Some approximate meaning seeping from. *Tin Wreath* #26 Wi 93
Some birds. *Wormwood Rev* 21(3):59 81
Some family relations. *Intrepid* #6 66
Some finality or other. *Intrepid* #7 Mr 67
Some fine panthers. *Simbolica* #31:14 [63?]
Some fucking thing—like a. *Shockbox* #4:21 92
Some had a conception of poetry as. *Blind Horse Rev* #3:24 Ag/Se 93
Some in belief. *St. Andrews Rev* 1(3):65 Fa/Wi 71
Some intent, presumably conscious, has. *Tandava* v14:14 My 88
Some kind /of purgatory. *Wormwood Rev* 21:3 81
Some Monday. *Wormwood Rev* 21:3 81
Some of the silences were what. *MAT*
Some poets presume metaphor as. *Ash* #7:28 Sp 91
Some quay beside some torrential. *Wormwood Rev* 27(4):93 87
Some sight of maybe moon. *Wormwood Rev* 5(2):31 65
Some smoke. *Wormwood Rev* 21(3):61 81
Some sort /of dawn. *Ab Intra* #1:22 72
Some strange words. *Wind* 4(14):11 74
Some substance. *GMV; NC; TDV*
Some who are slightly ascetic. *YMAN*
Some wonder why I need fantasy. *Chiron Rev* 12(1):11 Sp 93

Somehow it /seems almost your. *Blank Gun Silencer* #4:24 Sp 92

Something new /perchance. *S*

Something that wouldn't compute—. *Raw Bone* #4:10 Wi 85

Song for the times, A. *Naked Ear* #4 [57?]

Song /Pause. *AFTT; Crescendo* 2(3/4):20 Wi/Sp 43

Song within me, The. *Arx* 2(2):38 Jn 68

Sonic mass forth running. *MHC*

Soporific. *Crescendo* 1(4):11 Sp 42

Sought. *Arx* #11:37 Mr 68

Sources of ritual, The. *Curled Wire Chr* 2(4):8 Ja/Fe 55

South Anapuma Circle. *YMAN; Neo* Fa 53

Spacial canopy, The. *See:* Special canopy, star dreamed, The

Spanish heart for sleep for well. *YMAN*

Sparse saeson. [C.F.] *Free Lance* 2(2):11 54

Spate ringer singing Hi-ho. *Galley Sail Rev* #9:5 Fa 61

Special canopy, star dreamed, The. *N; South Dakota Rev* 10(4):5 Wi
72/73

Speckled speckled dove. *PB; Po Book Mag* 1(2) Wi 49

Spectre, The. *FSAB; Naked Ear* #1 [Wi 56]

Spikes are standing like sabres, The. *CCM*

Spiking the moist velvet. *Talisman (Lincoln:Neb.)* #1:14 73

Spilling recalcitrant loss. *IBG; Also* #2:59 Sp 51

Spine some facile dame. *OWH; Coastlines* #11:13 At 58

Spinner's contractable wheel, The. *Fallout* v2 Ag 63

Spinning. *Star-web Paper* #8:9 84

Spitting. *N; TM; Red Clay Reader* #2 65

Spontaneous forfeiture. *Embryo* 1(1):34 Jan 54

Sportin' high an' fine. *See:* Sport in high in fine

Sport in high in fine. *IBG; Inferno* #1:16 [51?]

Spot the leper his sin let sun. *MHC*

Spots of lone west. *White Dove Rev* #3 59

Spring betime. *Intrepid* #3 Jl 64

Spring in plummet in plume. *Grist* #5:18 Ap 65

Spring night. *Chameleon* Sp 37

Spring on the Texas prairie in. *Rocky Mountain Rev* 4(1):3,9 Fa 39

Springerwood and darling Janey. *Po Fund J* 1(1) Sp 60

Spurn the last cannon of fear. *Head* #2 65

Squash blossoms in silver, by the hun-. *GMV; Aura* #20:62 Sp 86

Staid. *NC; Renaissance* #1:cover 62
Stalemate. *Goodly Co.* #10:15 Nv 67
Stambole, stambole. *IBG; Simbolica* #14 [54?]
Standing up in bed. *Po nl (Philad.)* #10   66.
Start, The. *Bleb* #3 Jun 71
Starting at the beach. *SP*
Starting somewhere. *Greenfield Rev* 1(4):51 Sp 71
Startled, The. *NC*
Stated simply. *Wormwood Rev* 5(3):19 65
Statement on violence. *NN; Interim* 2(3/4):47 46
Statue, The. *Blue Grass* #2:25 Wi 63
Sterile plateau. *OWH; UWNB*
Stigmata. *Gale* 1(11):2 De 49
Still life by Braque. *Latitudes* 2(3):43 Su/Fa 70
Still life with orange. *IBG; Phoenix (Atlanta)* 2(1):25 55.
Stommer Bulltoven Crown. *AP; HNH; TWBS; Accent* 13(4):262 At 53
Stone, The. *Span* Su 42
Stone over. *NC*
Stones and the stars I have, The. *Dog River Rev* 10{2):24 Fa/Wi 91
Storm potential. *Howling Mantra* 91
Storm, The. *Wormwood Rev* 13(4):73 73
Storm of sand, not like fog—, A. *CM*
Storm of unfaithful intrusions—, A. *Fell Swoop* #26/27 [92?]
Strange tundra. *N; NN; Tiger's Eye* #7:7 [49?]
Strange unknown city. *N; PLS; Whispers* Mr 42
Strange woman. [W.E.B.] *Miscellaneous Man* #2:19 Su 54
Stranger, A. *N.*
Stranger, strange heart. [C.F.] *Deer and Dachshund* 1(2) [52?]
Strangest, The. *Wormwood Rev* 21(3):52 81
Street scene. *Simbolica* #22:5 [62]
Strength of any inconsequential, The. *Wormwood Rev* 31(4):122 91
Strictly, if all the excess. *BDS; GMV; Stone Drum* 1(6):20 Sp 88
Striped goards. *YCSW*
Strong-Heart is no fictional character. He is. *TH*
Stubble of charred forest, A. *Wormwood Rev* 24(1):9 84
Stunned sufficiently by the chalk-. *Plastic Tower* #6:2 Mr 91
Substance of the clown's story, The. *Blank Gun Silencer* #6:26 Sp 93
Subsuming the consistency that posits. *MAT*

Succinct, The. *NC*
Summer is over. *Aldebaran Rev* #2:16 68
Summer reaf the high the low. *MHC*
Summer romance. *El Coqui* #1:44 Ca 77/78
Summer storm that drove us beneath, A. *MAT*
Summer's half song, A. *Oak Leaves* 1(7) Jl 59
Sun and the absence of it. *YMAN; Simbolica* #21:1 [61?]
Sunrise. *Madrona* 3(8):29 74
Sunspots. *MS* #7 Wi 42
Suppose tomorrow. *VRG; Wormwood Rev* 15(2):62 75
Surfaces. *McLean County Po Rev* 2(1):7 Fa/Wi 76
Surging blood dispelled, The. *CCM; Matrix* Fa/Wi 47
Survival is not an objective I. *TDV; Puerto del Sol* 21(1):114 Su 85
Survivors, The. *HNH; Flame* 1(2):5 Su 54
Suspended. *NC*
Sutter's Canyon in half key light. *Sum* #1:19 De 63
Swabbie wan satchel ayne. *Wordjock* #4 Nv 68
Swans. *Blackbird Circle* #4:14 Sp 73
Swathed in white—not as a bride. *TH*
Sweep-down of tawny grasses as if, The. *GMV; Wind* 16(57):7 86
Sword the fallow lain in reason. *HPH*
Symbiosis. *S*
Systems, aforesaid. [C.F.] *Struggle* 1(1) Fe 54
Tain legge able sung. *Galley Sail Rev* #12:17 63
Take a woman he told me and you have taken poison. *AP*
Take care. *Wormwood Rev* 21(3):85 81
Taking notice of some nostalgic. *Guts* #6 89
Tame. *Scree* #5:26 76
Tammy Hacker chews tobacco. She. *Wormwood Rev* 31(4):125 91
Tankard, The. *YMAN; Simbolica* #10 53
Taos. *Po Taos* [#1] 57
Tedium. How interesting other. *Wormwood Rev* 31(4):125 91
Telegram, The. *Wormwood Rev* 24{2):73 84
Tell me of the hells you went through. *Chiron Rev* 12(1):1 Sp 93
Tepid tea since the samovar would not. *Wormwood Rev* 26(3):82 86
Testament for days to come. *Bozart-Westminster* Su 39
That cunt. *Wormwood Rev* 21(3):77 81
That diet cock, lite, that never cums. *Another Chicago Mag* #21 90

That girl I liked who became. *Black Gun Silencer* #3:10   Wi 91/92
That goose. *MOS*
That great, gross statue of a woman. *Wormwood Rev* 31(4):128   91
That hat /on. *BDS; Puerto del Sol* v16:19   Sp 81
That he should live so long. *Desperado* #7   72
That hoax the mind perpetrates. *Dog River Rev* 6(1):22   Sp 87
That insidious skin of resentment. *Blind Horse Rev* #3:23   Ag/Se 93
That it persists seems to constitute. *Wicked Mystic* #16:16   Ap 92
That key-. *Giants Play Well in the Drizzle* #26(4)   Jl 90
That large-mouthed. *Nausea* 9:40   Fa 75.
That portmanteau you are. *Post Motel* #6 [92?]
That quaint. *Po Now* #36:2   82
That railroad crossing we got stalled on. *No Mag* #7:13   87
That strong. *CYAM; HO; T; THYM*
That vivid. *Bitterroot* #92:56   Wi 87/88
That was what Louise liked most about Paul Goodman. *BDS*
Thaw, The. *Arx* #12:29   Ap 68
Their message. *N*
Then the children came, scattering. *CM; Star-web Paper* #8:9   84
Theological note. *Signet* 3(4):6   Ap 61
There are /many voices. *Wormwood Rev* 21(3):75   81
There are rooms beyond rooms—I can. *AAW*
There are salt marches here that seem to. *Amelia* 3(2):91   Sp 86
There are some prongs insidious to rub. *TH*
There are two kinds of people possessed. *Hippo* p17   Sp/Su 90
There is a belief that what is wrong with. *Guts* #6   89
There is that damp slight smear on. *Impetus* Male#2:30   Ag 90
There was this rat-haven I lived in. *Planet Detroit* #4/5:25   Sp 85
There were Ides of change, so to speak. *GMV; Writers Forum* 13   87
There were other places we had. *CM; HO; Beloit Po J* 33(3):7   Sp 83
These suicidal caresses—is that what. *Interim* 8(1):40   Sp 89
These wheels. *Wormwood Rev* 15(4):157   75
They are still . *N; Lemming* #1:11   Wi 71
They drove them out. *CM; Atom Mind* 3(11):63   Su 93
They've filled the world with them—babies. *Guts* #6   89
Thighs thin as popsicles. How many. *S*
Thing and essence. *Grande Ronde Rev* 1(1)   Fa 64
Things my hands have closed upon, The. *Wicked Mystic* #17:46   Je 92

This cat, Richard. *Lemming* #2:13 Wi 72
This cunt of yours. *La-bas* #4 Nv 76
This day, like festering flowers. *IBG*
This empty shibboleth—God become. *MAT; Ash* #8:14 Su 91
This filth. *SK*
This guarded epiphany that grabbed me. *Lactuca* #14(36) My 91
This guy. *Blackberry* #10:26 Su 79
This is the nub of it, you force your. *Wormwood Rev* 26(3):84 86
This is /the place. *NC*
This old stallion is restless, pacing. *Crab Creek Rev* 7(2):28 Su 91
This our brother in love. *Potpourri* 1:3 Sp 65
This ruin by moonlight. *WWSL; Imagi* 4(1):11 [48?]
This view of things was. *CM*
This was my happy childhood. *Gale* 1(3):1-6 My II 49
This wheel. *NC*
Those ones where fields once flourished. *Third Lung Press* #4(4) 89
Those parcelled. *Stone Country* 74(1):3 74
Those random skeletons I never be-. *Wicked Mystic* #19:26 Nv 92
Those spines. *CM; T*
Though I was /found in the. *Pembroke Mag* #3:34 72
Though literally true it is also symbolic of. *Ash* #6:27 Wi 91
Though /she had. *Wormwood Rev* 21(3):67 81
Though the apple be devoured. *HNH; OWH; Window* #6:2 53
Though the water. *Wind* 11(42):10 81
Though the world shudder not on the. *YMAN; Simbolica* #7 [53?]
Though we harbour. *CYAM; HO; THYM; Smudge* #4:56 Wi 79
Thoughts on returning. *SH*
Three brilliant. *Black Bear Rev* 1(3):68 Fa 75
Three little cherubs' rosy, The. *AFTT; Fiddlehead* #62:12 Fa 64
Three remote afternoons. *N; PB; Po NY* #1:13 49
Through all the San Joaquin area. *CM*
Through these monuments the sky has. *TDV; Studio One* p14 Sp 86
Through work. *Encore* 5(1):4 At 70
Thumbing through a stack of this new. *Gypsy* #12/13:55 89
Thus now the smooth low mound. *OWH; Embryo* 1(1):32 Jan 54
Thus we fly, inch by inch, out. *Fell Swoop* #26/27 [92?]
Ticonderoga and Tippecanoe. *PB; Line* 1(3) 49
Tight steward, The. *UWNB; Fresco* ns#1:61 [Fa] 60

Tight-clenched as a clam on a rock. *Paper Bag* 2(1):9 Wi 89/90
Time diversion. *Grist* #5:20 Ap 65
Time for prayer. *Wormwood Rev* 5(3):21 65
Time for prayer, Brothers, Berryman. *GMV; Interim* 5(2):11 Fa 86
Time has come when I do not par-, The. *TH*
Time piece. *UWNB*
Tip, The. *NC; Po Now* #26:22 80
Tit mold. *Centering* #1 [73?]
Tital-tattle-ation. *Existaria* #7:16 Se/Oc 57
Titles of resignation, The. *CYAM; IINH; HO; THYM; Inferno* #9:7 53
To a frigid nymph. *Compass* #12:32 [49?]
To a girl I like. *SP*
To a wicked woman. *Mag* #5:51 73
To be precise. If I cut the ice—with. *S*
To breathe. *Wormwood Rev* 15(2):63 75
To carry. *Wormwood Rev* 15(4):157 75
To catch. *T*
To clean out a tunnel. *From a Window* #3 Oct 65
To die to give freedom back again. *S*
To finish out a line or meter once. *GMV*
To follow a fugue tenuously dancing. *Crab Creek Rev* 7(2):28 Su 91
To get a Guggenheim you have to be a. *BDS; NYQ* #39:68 Su 89
To invoke—to revoke. If my head is up-. *Studio One* p16 Sp 91
To make an exit. *YMAN*
To make judgments of a less judgmental. *NYQ* #44:49 91
To never see [C.F.] *DB; TM; Free Lance* 3(1):8 55
To one dead in prison. *Crescendo* 2(3/4):8 Wi/Sp 43
To pound. *Black Gun Silencer* #3:10 Wi 91/92
To put a rose upon it. *Po Rev (Tampa)* #2 64
To resolve. *Wormwood Rev* 21(3):61 81
To return /again. *Margarine Maypole* #63 Je 84
To saints their sainthood. *HO; CYAM; THYM*
To seed is to bleed. *TM*
To trace the disease back to its in-. *AAW*
To winter the mind. *TWBS; Po Book Mag* 3(2):7 Wi 51
To wring some water out. *Grist* #8:5 66
Today's hostage. *VB*
Together /in bed. *Wormwood Rev* 15(2):67 75

Unspecial mirth, An. *White Dove Rev* #3 59
Untamed, not so much as an unstalked, The. *Stone Drum* 1(4):19 86
Untitled poem /But we could speak to. *AP; SCV; Atom Mind* 3(11):59
     Su 93
Up to. *Washout Rev* #3:51 Sp 76
Upholstered winter of white snow, The. *BDS; Open 24 Hours* #7 91
Vampire hunt. *Po Fund J* 1(4) Sp 61
Vase, The. *Elizabeth* #13:27 Jl 69
Venus sucking the night now, wheeling. *S*
Vet, The. *Gum* #6 Sep 71
Vilely I have taken. *Blitz* [#2?] [64?]
Virgin heart, The. *IBG; Archer* 3(4):16 Wi 53/54
Virgin presumptuous. *Whetstone (Huntsville, TX)* 2(1):15 Fa 68
Vision of, The. *NC*
Visions. *MC; NC*
Visitation, A. *Star-web Paper* #6:31 77
Visitor, The. *Wormwood Rev* 13(2):72 73
Visuals, The. *Harvest* #43:95 Fa 79
Voscum Meade the middy mons. *AP; Deer and Dachshund* #4 [53?]
Vulley valen twine. *AP*
Wager, The. *Grande Ronde Rev* #14.75 Sp 73
Wail, o wind from the west. *Westminster* 34(4):9 Wi 45
Wain sordid drill is May. *CCM; Rough Weather* #1:6 Fa 50
Wake. *Blue beat* p6 Mr 64
Wake up. [T.D.] *Curled Wire Chr* 2(3):7 Nv 54
Waking at dawn. *Simbolica* #24:18 [62?]
Waking in an unfamiliar place, not. *MAT*
Wall, The. *Lost & Found Times* #12 Oc 82
Walpurgis night. *El Coqui* #2:34 Ta 78
War is kind. *Flame* 7(4):17 Wi 60
War poem. [T.D.] *Struggle* 1(2) Mr 54
War, The. *N*
War year: 1943. *IBG; P; Points* #18:63 Wi 53/54
Warped returning, A. *AAW*
Warthog rooten. *Arx* 2(3):56 Jl 68
Was I ever welcomed? To the womb. *Pearl* #17:68 Sp 93
Was it her garter-belt hanging on. *Ash* #8:14 Su 91
Was it through all the San Juaquin area. *Po Now* #36:3 82

Watching a brindle spotted dog. *N*
Water /images in three. *Conditioned Response* #8:4 [88?]
Waters, The. *Another Chicago Mag* #6 81
Wattle, A. *Wild Dog* #2:9 Ap 63
Way she fucked was like, The. *Experiment in Words* 3(9):13 92
Way-station off Pernambuco. *TWBS; Free Lance* 2(1):26 54
We ate green apples and heaved. *CM*
We danced off. *Wormwood Rev* 15(2):66 75
We grew. *Wormwood Rev* 15(2):65 75
We have known. *HPH; Wormwood Rev* 2(3):3 62
We need a Republican administration. *Input* 1(3) Se 64
We sat down on the white, hot dunes. *Raw Bone* #4:10 Wi 85
We took a slow trip to the backwaters. *Innisfree* 12(4):40 My 93
We were fetched by a small. *GMV; Another Chicago Mag* #15 86
Weal in apple drilling. *Erratica* 1(4):24 73
Weather green coiffure, The. *Galley Sail Rev* #9:6 Fa 61
Weep not the age. *Simbolica* #18 [60?]
Weep the mulberry ladder. *HPH; Signet* 3(9):4 Oc 61
Weight of kisses that strangles us, The. *Aileron* 12:8 91
Weirwoman. *Crescendo* 1(4):10 Sp 42
Well, anyhow . *Atom Mind* #6:17 Fa 69
Wellen wrested in bold ripe flame. *Dasein* #7/8 68
Wells of dread. *Dasein* #7/8 68
Wellsprings of night. *FSAB; Miscellaneous Man* #2:19 Su 54
Went out. *Wormwood Rev* 21(3):50 81
West cold leaf of mumble. *MHC*
West like the iceman's dawn. *HPH; Signet* 3(9):4 Oc 61
Westerow Bulltoven Mel. *AP; Deer and Dachshund* #4 [53?]
Wet pavement. *Wisconsin Rev* 6(3):15 Su 71
What a price. *Illuminations* #4 Wi 68/69
What am I looking for when I walk into. *MAT*
What are you /going to do. *It* #5 My 66
What arrows were shot as a warning—. *Howling Mantra* 91
What Babylon was built. *CCM; N; WWSL; TWBS; Po* 83(5):258 Fe 54
What goes on inside. *CM; TDV; Another Chicago Mag* #9 83
What has been /my response. *N; Star-web Paper* #6:30 77
What helmsman. *Sunset Palms Hotel* 4(7) Wi 76
What I /have backed away from. *YCSW*

What is her vulva really like—a tiger-. *NYQ* #43:44 Fa 90
What is "my case against women" in. *Blind Horse Rev* #3:23 Ag/Se 93
What is /your flower. *Wildflower* #2 De 81
What kind of a doll was this doll? She had. *TH*
What tumult, what strife uninterred. *Raven Anth* #71:9 Ja 47
What was the root of my undoing? Ah. *Howling Mantra* 91
What will /it be. *Wormwood Rev* 21(3):81 81
Wheel driven. [C.F.] *SScribe* p50 [57?]
Wheel was a wheel before that Aztec, The. *Ash* #6:12 Wi 91
Wheels within wheels. *CCM*
When at last unshelved. *Harlequin* 4(1):4 Sp 67
When did the changes come—not as if. *S*
When eminent domain decreed. *Wormwood Rev* 31(4):123 91
When enter the rain. *IBG; Simbolica* #10 53
When I compose myself for sleep on. *MAT*
When I /was. *Wormwood Rev* 15(2):70 75
When it is over, when it has gotten to be. *Rag Mag* 11(1):40 93
When since /nineteen. *Goodly Co.* #4:5 De 65
When we /Anima speaks: *Purr* #4 76
When we were young. *N; FSAB; Yugen* #1:8 58
When you crouch. *Grande Ronde Rev* #14.75 Sp 73
When you /open. *Wormwood Rev* 21(3):73 81
Where in Konarak. *SK*
Where it's put together. *Wine Rings* 1(2):7 [75?]
Where prevention began. *Earthjoy* #2 72
Where that we are taken. *Whetstone (Huntsville, TX)* 2(1):17 Fa 68
Where /the flesh. *NC*
Where the heavy. *Grimoire* #4:19 Sp 83
Where the will resides. *Wild Dog* #7:12 Ap 64
Where /was I. *NC; Atom Mind* 3(11):59 Su 93
Where we embrace. *AFTT; N; Fiddlehead* #64:11 Sp 65
Where we laundered our linen was. *MAT; i: the First Person* #4:19 91
Where we /were not intended. *N; T*
Where you /have not. *Minotaur* #8:34 83
Whether /the upshot. *Thirteen* 5(4):4 Jl 87
Whether the vagina is as cave-like. *AAW*
While /getting. *Wormwood Rev* 21(3):79 81
Whine Morger fasting on light. *SCV; WWSL; Three Hands* #4 52

Whirlwind restless for, A. *New Writing from Zambia* 10(3):2   Oc 74
Whisper no lion is gear. *Theo* 1(1)   [Sp 64?]
Whistle the moon, the baying hounds. *Goliards* #5:31   Jl 65
Whit-. *Wormwood Rev* 22(4):146   82
White and purple. *Road Apple Rev* 4(4):30   Wi 73
White /as your flesh. *TM; Red Clay Reader* #2   65
White birds. *Foxfire* 3(3):39   Wi 69
White constancy *PB; Berkeley* #7:7   49
White heron again calling, The. *AFTT*
White hollyhocks. *YMAN; Yugen* #4:13   Sp 59
White is our color for love. *P; UWNB; Cleveland Rev* 1(2)   Wi/Sp 92
White lily—white. *TM*
White mother. *Mati* #4:90   Wi/Sp 77
White token. *CCM; Imagi* 4(1):10   [48?]
White water. Is that where we are. *CM*
White whale, the white, The. *HNH; N; Beloit Po J* 8:2:19   Wi 57/58
Who am I, among these, she asked. *Free Lunch* #11:22   Wi 93
Who ever dreamed of being warm? Hell. *Shockbox* 1(6):4   [93?]
Who has ever thought of me as going. *Minotaur* #25/26:11   91
Who knew not beauty. *Westminster* 38(1):18   Sp 49
Who knows. *Centering* #1   [73?]
Who seeks a constant lover. *Crescendo* 1(4):9   Sp 42
Who steadfastly court the anguish, the tears. *Crescendo* 1(4):9   Sp 42
Who traveled fastest and. *Blind Horse Rev* #1:27   Jl 92
Why angered in the gentle dawn. *Quetzal* 1(1):7   Sep 70
Why do people live. [C.F.] *Suck-egg Mule* #1   [51?]
Why does the squirrel chase his own. *Thunder Sandwich* #3   85
Why hide it? Walter said to Meadow. *Bonesauce* #8:10   [89?]
Widowhood in heeding wonder, A. *CM*
Wild frizzle of your frighted hair, The. *Bonesauce* #8:17   [89?]
Wild one, The. *Outcast* #15   69
Will to lie down, The. *Existaria* #2:5   [5-?]
Wind. *NC*
Wind, The. *Wormwood Rev* 21(3):69   81
Wind funeral. [T.D.] *Deer and Dachshund* 1(1)   Sp 51
Windows I have stared out of looking. *Lactuca* #12:37   Fe 89
Winged bird, A. *Moment* #12:37   89
Wings of an angry eaglet which. *GMV*

Winning. *N; Literary Artpress* 2(1):34 Fa 60
Winter edge. *OWH; Po* 93(3):157 De 58
Winter vacation. *Wormwood Rev* 3(2):18 63
Winter winter swift as arrow. *Head* #2 65
Wisdom is silent. [C.F.] *Suck-egg Mule* #1 [50?]
With a distant slight smile, my driver. *Raw Bone* #4:11 Wi 85
With a rope of gold. *NN; Approach* #4:27 48
With all of my tainted beginnings and. *AAW*
With butterflies. *El Coqui* #2:36 Ta 78
With its own hands. *PLS*
With my /hands over my balls. *Spirit that Moves Us* 1(3):38 My 76
With no /penetration. *Minotaur* #7:8 83
With only /a little. *Wormwood Rev* 21(3):86 81
With remorse. *VRG; Wormwood Rev* 15(2):61 75
With some straining. *Po Eastwest* #4:30 71
With three. *El Coqui* #2:35 Ta 78
With what mad, pell-mell redundancies. *Tandava* Ja 91
With your eyes. *Star-web Paper* #6:30 77
Within a high building overlooking the. *OWH; Hearse* #3:26 [58]
Withold. *Showcase* #2:8 Nv/De 65
Without imp-. *Wind* 11(42):9 81
Without presuming. *S*
Woman of the willows, The. *UWNB; Prairie Schooner* #33:323 Wi
    59/60
Word by wind. *Wormwood Rev* 21(3):75 81
Words and the tone are surely, The. *AAW*
World from the pelvic arch. *HPH; NDCN; PB; Bridge* Sup#1:12 48
Worthless leven rose in flux. *Spearhead* 2(2):24 Sp 51
Would it have pleased either of us. *Wormwood Rev* 31(4):129 91
Would you call it dynamite?—or is it. *AAW*
Wreath for the fathers. *Curled Wire Chr* 2(4):8 Ja/Fe 55
Wreath /of roses, A. *Thirteen* 5(4):4 Jl 87
Wreath silent held. *AFTT*
Wren caged. *White Arms* [#1] Ap 74
Wrest over. *Wild Dog* #7:11 Ap 64
Writing poetry. *N; Riverrun* 1(4) 67
Writing, writing—Henry Miller. *Wind* 17(61):6 87
Yes, I /kissed. *Post Motel* #4 [92?]

Yes if /I had to. *Wormwood Rev* 21(3):56 81
Yes, you, among some. *Mutated Viruses* #11:78 [92?]
Yet long may live. *NN; Voices* #135:9 At 48
You are adorned. *SK*
You are /flashing there. *Po Nl (Scranton)* #11 [66?]
You can take /politics. *NDCN*
You clasped your hands. *CM; Atom Mind* 3(11):63 Su 93
You could say I had not been. *GMV; Old Red Kimono* v15:53 Sp 86
You crazy fellow. *Harlequin* v5:29 Wi 68
You don't /have. *Wormwood Rev* 21:3 81
You get what you ask for. *PLS*
You have invaded my dreams, my ul-. *Blank Gun Silencer* #7:46 93
You, Sissy, had found the bright stone. *Guts* #7:15 Christmas 89
You surprised me, moving back on this. *Dog River Rev* 5(2):6 At 86
You think that is Bulltoven etherized. *Blind Horse Rev* #3:22 Ag/Se 93
You took my clothes off of me. *GMV; Oro Madre* 2(3/4):16 84
You with /your language. *GMV; Studio One* p16 Sp 86
You would like. *Wormwood Rev* 13(2):71 73
You /Yvor Winters. *South Florida Po J* #4/5:187 70
You're symbolic. *T*
You've always had crow's feet at the. *Plastic Tower* #13:22 De 92
Young man with spats, The. *NN; NM Q Rev* 16(3):352 At 46
Your answer. [C.F.] *Naked Ear* #3 [57?]
Your ass. *MOS*
Your body. *SK*
Your broad. *NC*
Your buck. *Second Coming* 7(1):11 79
Your cock. *Egg/Surfside Po Rev* 1(3):28 Su 73
Your cracked hero worship for men. *Wormwood Rev* 26(3):86 86
Your cunt is /slightly dry. *Wildflower* #37 Je 4 86
Your cunt /is virginal. *Open 24 Hours* #5:3 86
Your cunt /may be a sow's ear. *Wormwood Rev* 15(2):63 75
Your cunt /miraculous. *Purr* #3 75
Your cunt /seems twice as large. *BDS*
Your de-. *NC*
Your existence. *N; Wormwood Rev* 15(2):67 75
Your eyes. *NC*
Your hand /among. *Bonesauce* #8:10 [89?]

Your hands open and fragile as leaves. *Fell Swoop* #25 [92?]
Your heroic. *Scree* #2 74
Your knees. *Wormwood Rev* 21(3):84 81
Your legs. *BDS; NYQ* #40:68 Fa 89
Your little. *Scree* #3 75
Your long legs. *Star-web Paper* #6:31 77
Your maiden. *S*
Your naked /legs. *Harvest* #43:94 Fa 79
Your opaque. *Nausea One* 11(6):14 Sp 74
Your pencil. *S*
Your placid /eyes, great. *SK*
Your platinum eyes and bronze. *Lactuca* #14:37 My 91
Your real. *S*
Your serene face. *SK*
Your slender. *CYAM; THYM; NM Humanities Rev* 3(1):39 Sp 80
Your tapestry. *NC*
Your thighs. *CYAM; HO; THYM; UWNB; Epos* 12(2):21 Wi 60
Your tits in. *Purr* #3 75
Your uncluttered. *Egg/Surfside Po Rev* 1(3):29 Su 73
Your white /body in. *Kindred Spirit* 7(3):7 Wi 88/89
Youth but age redundant. *HPH; Emergent* #5 58
Zebra of intention, A. *NDCN*

Number of poems published in little magazines by year

1937	4	1956	14	1975	70
1938	2	1957	33	1976	32
1939	4	1958	24	1977	24
1940	1	1959	24	1978	7
1941	14	1960	22	1979	18
1942	14	1961	31	1980	26
1943	5	1962	14	1981	90
1944	1	1963	33	1982	24
1945	3	1964	48	1983	28
1946	13	1965	66	1984	25
1947	9	1966	27	1985	41
1948	17	1967	27	1986	39
1949	27	1968	32	1987	36
1950	32	1969	29	1988	26
1951	38	1970	31	1989	63
1952	24	1971	28	1990	36
1953	44	1972	40	1991	67
1954	50	1973	54	1992	54
1955	46	1974	29	1993	52
1937-55	348	1956-74	606	1975-93	758

The productive periods: 1953-55, 1964-65, 1972-75 (except 1974), 1985-87, and especially 1989-93.

Book Reviews of

Score for this Watch by James Franklin Lewis. *Crescendo* 1(1) Se 41
An Examination of Ezra Pound, ed. Peter Russell *Suck-egg mule* #5 [51?]
The Autobiography of William Carlos Williams. Suck-egg Mule #5 [51?]
Selected Poems by Oscar Williams. *Prairie Schooner* v33:202,266-9 59
Book Selection and Censorship by Marjorie Fisk. *Horsefly* Je 9 60.
Tripping in America by John Bennett. *Pembroke Mag* #20:289 88

[by T.D.]

Three roads to the sun [review of *Beloved Kinsman and Other Poems* by
K.L. Beaudoin, *City Hall Street* by Raymond Suster, and *The Furious
Finding* by Frederic Vanson]. *Deer and dachshund* 1(1) Sp 51

[by C.F.]

Acts of ego and acts of love [review of *Strange April* by Beaudoin, *The
Sensual Image* by Pearl Bond, and *Mussolini has Met is End in the Mad
House* by M.J. Mason]. *Deer and Dachshund* 1(3) [53?]

Autobiographical

Shoe string publisher. *Southwestern American Lit* 11(1):5-15 Fa 85
From the memoirs of Judson Crews ["Up your nose..."]. *Gypsy* #15:22-25 90
From the memoirs of Judson Crews ["Up your nose..."]. *Coventry
Reader* 3(4) Wi 90/91
Henry Miller and my Big Sur Days: Vignettes from Memory. El Paso,
Vergin P., 1992.

Articles

A note on Mason Jordan Mason. *Bridge* 2(12):181-90 Ag 17 48
A note on [Mason Jordan] Mason's poetry. *Bridge* 4(4) Ja 1 50
A note on the dance. *Deer and Dachshund* 1(1) Sp 51

The glare of the living moment mirrored in the cauldron of the rose. *Deer and Dachshund* 1(2) [52?]
A note on obscenity in Henry Miller. *Deer and Dachshund* 1(3) [53?]
My first and last word on Hemingway (1939). *Deer and Dachshund* 1(3) [53?]
Two notes on Mason Jordan Mason. *Deer and Dachshund* #5 [54?]
Reply to [Ellen] Edelman. *Trace* #9:3 Oc 54
To Stefanile [letter to the Editor]. *Sparrow* #3 [55?]
Profile for the loving critic. *Trace* #55:331-2 My 65
From the Indian capitol of the world (critical essay). *HD* p89 72
[Advice to young poets: excerpt from a letter to the ed.]. *HD* p85 72
Letter from Lusaka/Letter to Norman. *Pembroke Mag* #7:336-9 76
Henry Miller and the millennial oranges of Big Sur. *Pembroke Mag* 16:160-6 84

[by C.F.]

Jacqueline Borgermill, Sybilline artist. *Deer and Dachshund* #5 [54?]

Fiction

Deportation. *Rocky Mountain Rev* 3(2):5,8 Wi 38/39
Maybe he was a poet. *Crescendo* 1(5) Su 42
The beginning of remembrance. *Crescendo* 2(1) At 42
Mute incalculable torrent. *Deer and Dachshund* 1(1) Sp 51
Cochise. *Center* #13:58 81

Interviews

Interview: Judson Crews (by Casanda Burleson Bell). *Whetstone* 4(1): 35-6 Sp 70

Audiocassettes

Two Readings by the Poet Judson Crews. [Recorded in Taos in the summers of 63 and 64 by Eric Bauersfeld.] Berkeley: KPFA, 64?]

[Judson Crews reading at the University of New Mexico, winter solstice. 71.] Unpubd.

The Ahsahta Cassette Sampler: 14 Western Poets Read from their Ahsahta Press Volumes. [Judson Crews reads 4 poems.] Boise: Ahsahta P., 83.

[Judson Crews, Diana Huntress and Arden Tice reading at the Unitarian Church of Albuq., August 16, 86.] Unpubd.

[Judson Crews reading from *Brave Bulltoven*, August 4, 88.] 2 cassettes. Unpubd.

[Judson Crews reading a selection of poems edited by Joanie Whitebird but never published. August 10, 88.] Unpubd.

[Judson Crews reading *Nations and people*, August 12, 88.] Unpubd.

[Judson Crews reading miscellaneous unselected recent poems, August 12, 88.] Unpubd.

Conversation with Judson Crews, and Belinda Subraman, S. Ramnath, Wendell B. Anderson. El Paso: Vergin P., c91.

[Judson Crews interviewed, November 17, 91.] Unpubd.

Manuscript Sources

The papers of Judson Crews may be consulted in the Special Collections departments of the libraries of the University of California at Los Angeles, the University of New Mexico, the University of Texas at Austin, and the Beinecke Library at Yale.

Unpublished works

(some not completed)

(Most of the works in this and the following section can be consulted at the Humanities Research Center, University of Texas, Austin, Texas)

Poetry

Cellar Door
The Dead Age, the Naked Earth
The Iron Crucible
Light, the Daemon Shroud
May Balls and Door of Vales (Poetry & dreams)

Stella Orbeture
Sudden Encounter

Fiction

I Have no Pleasure in Them (Novel)
A Tyranny of Tears (Novel)
Why Ask the Angry Gods? (Novel)
The Beginning of Remembrance (Short stories)

Other prose

An Annotation of the Eye: Poems of Kenneth L. Beaudoin (Literary criticism)
Mason Jordan Mason (Biography)
The Slow Redemption (Literary criticism)
The South of William Faulkner (An appreciation)
Studies in Courtship and Marriage (Sociology)
Tenets of Astro-psychiatry (Psychology)
The Tropics and the Myth of Cain (Literary criticism)
The Brave Wild Coast (Memoir)

SECONDARY SOURCES

Biographical

"Top censor taken to task by Judson Crews." [Comment]. *Dorian Book Q* 4th ¼ 60. With 2 letters of Judson Crews.

MacNab, Arden. "New Mexico profiles: Judson Crews." *New Mexican* (Santa Fe) Je 27 65; reptd. in her *Looking for the Frontier* (El Paso, Vergin P., 92), p. 34-37.

Foster, Joseph O'Kane. "Tribute to Judson Crews." *El Crepusculo* (Taos) Je-Jl 66.

The Little Magazine in America: a Modern Documentary History, ed. Elliott Anderson and Mary Kinzie. Yonkers, N.Y., Pushcart P., 78. (Especially p. 715-16, on *The Naked Ear*.)

"Judson Crews." *Poetry now* 6(6):[0]-2+ 82.

Murphey, J.C. [Review of M.J. Mason's *A Vehicle to Raise the Dead*.] *NM Humanities Rev* 5(2):89-91 Su 82.

Contemporary Authors, New Revision Series 7(10):130-31.

Anderson, Wendell B. *Big Sur: Primavera*. In *Pembroke Mag* #17   85; reptd. as a separate book (El Paso: Vergin P., 91).

Winslow, Kathryn. *Henry Miller: Full of Life* Los Angeles: Tarcher, 86.

Contemporary Authors Autobiography Series 14:101-19 91.

Smith, Gregory. *Atom Mind* 3(11): Su 93.

Analytical

In addition to the following references, several non-self-published collections of Crews' poems include analytical prefaces or afterwords by various writers.

Beaudoin, Kenneth Lawrence. *Crescendo* 1(4):13 Sp 42.

Greer, Scott. "The poetry of Trumbull Drachler [pseud. of Judson Crews]." *Deer and Dachshund* 1(1) Sp 51.

Coffield, Glen. *Criteria for Poetry* (Eagle Creek, OR: The author, 54), p. 144-5, 164-5.

Eckman, Frederick. "Neither tame nor fleecy." *Poetry* 90(6):386-97 Se 57.

Eckman, Frederick. Critique of "Cold for night and lasting." In his *Cobras and Cockle Shells* (West Lafayette, IN: Sparrow, 58), p. 30-1.

De Witt, G. "On Syntax in Poems," pt. 3. *Blue Guitar* #18 Sp 61.

Creeley, Robert. "Judson Crews." In *Desert Rev Anthology* (Santa Fe: Desert Review P., 74), p. 5.

Mantis, Peter. "Judson Crews, fuck yeah!" *Antenna* #1:24-30 89.

Book Reviews

The Anatomy of Proserpine. Whetstone 1(2):106-7 Su 55.

The Anatomy of Proserpine, rev. by Hugh Kenner. *Poetry* 86(4):244-7 Jl 55.

Angels Fall, They are Towers. SDR [?], 4(1):107 Sp 66.

Angels Fall, They are Towers, rev. by Thomas Clark. *Poetry* 108(6):408-15 Se 66.

Angels Fall, They are Towers, rev. by Douglas Blazek. *Latitudes* 1(1) Fe 67.

Blood Devisable by Sand. Plastic tower #9:39 De 91.

Come Curse to the Moon, rev. by John Forbis. *Experiment* 6(2):63 52.

The Feel of Sun and Air upon her Body. Trace #36:42 Mr/Ap 60.

The Feel of Sun and Air upon her Body, rev. by Robert Creeley. *Poetry* 98(3):198 Je 61.

The Heart in Naked Hunger, rev. by Robert Creeley. *Poetry* 98(3):198 Je 61.

Henry Miller and my Big Sur Days, rev. by Laurence Hawkins. *Dog River Rev* #22:45 92

Henry Miller and my Big Sur Days, rev. by Brian Clark. *Puck* #9:63 Wi 92/93

Henry Miller and my Big Sur Days, rev. by Catherine Lynn. *Chiron Rev* 12(1):18-19 Sp 93

Henry Miller and my Big Sur Days, rev. by Shelby Stephenson. *Pilot* p2-B Ap 19 93.

Henry Miller and my Big Sur Days, rev. by Michael Thurston. *Coal City Rev* #7:51 93

Henry Miller and my Big Sur Days, rev. by Ron Androla. *Bogg Reviews* #66:16 93

Hermes Past the Hour, rev. by Winfield Townley Scott. *New Mexican* (Santa Fe) Oc 20 63.

Hermes Past the Hour. Free Lance 8(1):28 64.

Hermes Past the Hour, rev. by Douglas Blazek. *Ole* #1 64.

Hermes Past the Hour, rev. by Spencer Brown. *Chelsea* #15:118 Je 64.

Hermes Past the Hour, rev. by Dabney Stuart. *Poetry* 104(4):258-64 Jl 64.

Hermes Past the Hour, rev. by Ben L. Hiatt. *Grande Ronde Rev* 1(1):23 Fa 64.

Inwade to Briney Garth, rev. by Spud Johnson. *Horsefly* v.13:45 60.

Inwade to Briney Garth, rev. by L.W. Michaelson. *Midwest* #2:31-2 Su 61.

No is the Night. Imagi 5(2):23 50.

The Ogres who were his Henchmen. Trace #37:44 My/Je 60.

The Ogres who were his Henchmen, rev. by Henry Birnbaum. *Poetry* 97(2):114-20 Nv 60.

A Poet's Breath, rev. by Arthur Merims. *Intro* 1(2):106 50?

A Poet's Breath. Gryphon Fa 50.

Psalms for a Late Season, rev. by Scott Greer. *Crescendo* 1(5):15-16 Su 42.

The Stones of Konarak, rev. by Robert Vas Dias. *Poetry* 110(3):186-95 Je 67.

Three on a Match, rev. by Robert Van Dias. *Poetry* 110(3):186-195 Je 67.

To Wed Beneath the Sun, rev. by Frederick Eckman. *Poetry* 90(6):386-97 Se 57.

A Unicorn when Needs be. *Trace* #52:93 My 64.

A Unicorn when Needs be, rev. by Spencer Brown. *Chelsea* #15:118 Je 64.

A Unicorn when Needs be, rev. by R.P. Dickey. *Taos News* pC-6 Jl 11 91.

A Unicorn when Needs be. *Plastic Tower* #8:43 Se 91.

The Wrath Wrenched Spendor of Love, rev. by Frederick Eckman. *Poetry* 90(6):386-97 Se 57.

You, Mark Antony, Navigator upon the Nile, rev. by A.R. Ammons. *Poetry* 108(3):191-7 Je 66.

You, Mark Antony, Navigator upon the Nile, rev. by Douglas Blazek. *Latitudes* 1(1) Fe 67.

Tributes (Poems)

Greer, Scott. "Pearl Harbor Day, December 7, 1941, for Judson Crews." (Unpubd.)

Greer, Scott. "Augury /for J.C.C." 42.

Greer, Scott. "To Judson in Taos." *Suck-Egg Mule* #1 [51?]

Beaudoin, Kenneth Lawrence. "From letters for 7 exiled: iii. (for J.C. on the plains)" *Suck-Egg Mule* #1 [51?].

Atkins, John. "To Judson in chaos." *Suck-egg Mule* #3/4 [52?]

Smith, D.V. "It is mostly a matter of praise life--for anybody but: Judson Crews." *Wormwood Rev* 6(1):34-35 66.

Burlingame, Robert. "Sober poem (for Judson Crews)." At 66. (Unpubd.)

The Testimony of Henry Miller

The Judson Crews papers at UCLA contain (Box 3, folders 8-10) 96 letters from Henry Miller, written between October 1942 and November 1948. Several times Miller expressed admiration for Judson's writing. On August 10, 1944 he called a published Crews poem "fine," and on the 30th of the same month he deemed another "excellent." Of *The Southern Temper*, the first portion of his M.A. thesis for Baylor University, Henry said: "it knocks blazes out of my book on America" (*The Air-conditioned Nightmare*), and he submitted it on Judson's behalf to one of his own publishers, James Laughlin of New Directions.

Almost all of Miller's letters express deep appreciation to Judson, either for his personal friendship or for the immense amount of time he put into "business" on Henry's behalf. Henry was constantly asking him to look out for a copy of a book, sometimes one of his own to give or sell to a friend, more often a work by another author of whom he was currently enamored. Usually Judson found the book very quickly, eliciting from Miller the most generous expressions of gratitude and sometimes astonishment. Judson would also, on his own initiative, locate copies of Henry's books that were illegally circulating in the United States and lend them to his friends, a gesture which Henry called unprecedented in his experience.

The Testimony of Anaïs Nin

Fourteen letters from Anaïs Nin are found in the same box at UCLA. The subject matter is almost entirely Judson's attempts to sell Nin's works. The tone of the letters is unfailingly gracious, and increasingly appreciative of Judson for his efforts.

One refers to his poem, "Psalm for the Mortified Flesh." Of it she writes that it is "strong poetry, which grasps the mood and the body vigorously."

About the Author

Wendell Anderson has published poetry in the little magazines and university quarterlies since 1939/40, and in thirteen chapbooks. He established Buzzard's Roost Press in 1988 to preserve in chapbook form the poetry of his late wife, Emily F. Anderson, as well as his own and others'.

He has lived most of his life in New Mexico (especially Taos), and the rest of it in Idaho, Oregon, California, Montana and New Hampshire. He has worked as a patrolman on an antelope refuge, a forest fire control aide, a timber faller and loader, a log jack, a ski run cutter and a horse currier. He has also been an artist's model, a bookmobile operator, a hospital orderly and licensed practical nurse, a caseworker and social worker, and a teacher of creative writing.

He attended the University of Oregon, Reed College and Franklin Pierce College (Rindge, New Hampshire), where he wrote a thesis on the poetry of Judson Crews. For the last ten years he has been working on *Stono*, a long poem on the American West.

About the Editor

Jefferson P. Selth is Librarian Emeritus at the University of California, Riverside; he has also served in the Unitarian Universalist ministry. He has written books on librarianship, woman-man relationships, alternative lifestyles and Thomas Starr King, and is presently working on a biography of Etienne Dumont.

Index